FREE
WAY

an adventure
through loss

BY
RACHEL
HELDEN

Rachel
Helden

Published by Rachel Helden
www.rachelhelden.com

Rachel Helden
Free Way Project
9621 Olive Blvd.
PO Box 8311
St. Louis, MO 63132

First paperback edition October 2021

All text and photographs by Rachel Helden
Book cover design by Laura Grant Design
Book layout design by Olivia Leigh Smith and Heather Brown
Map by Rand McNally

Library of Congress Control Number: 2021915513

ISBN 978-0-578-87633-7 (paperback)
ISBN 978-0-578-96295-5 (ebook)
ISBN 978-0-578-96296-2 (audiobook)

Printed in the United States of America

In Loving Memory of my Dad,
George Bendall Helden
Who told me, "Don't let this year ruin your life,
turn it around for something good."

And for those radiant souls,
who passed on to the next life during the writing of these pages,
you have expanded my heart even more.
Grandpa Ray Peterson
Dave Heaton
Patti Trent

This book is an offering for anyone who is going through their own adventure through loss. Sending you love for your journey.

contents

SAE OW-20

2 **United States**

Capital: Washington, D-17
Land area: 3,531,905 sq. mi.

Selected National Park Service locations

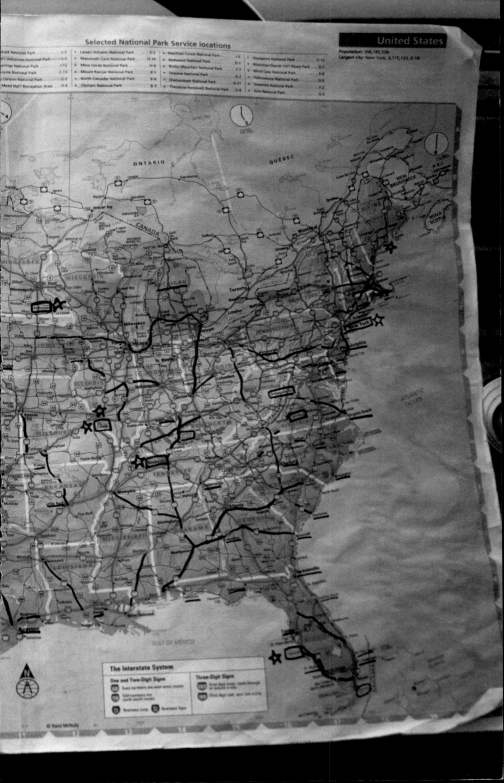

Selected National Park Service locations

Population: 308,745,538
Largest city: New York, 8,175,133, E-18

ONTARIO QUÉBEC

CANADA

The Interstate System

© Rand McNally

leaving

My mind blank, I could see what my hands were doing, but was unable to process it in that moment. I threw some clothes and toiletries into a bag, my laptop, and grabbed some books I had been meaning to read. What was essential in life snapped into focus when quickly packing a small bag. Gathering my purse and keys from a hook near the door, I began to float towards the car. I don't remember walking to it.

Somehow I had become scared to be in my own home. *How on earth did it get to this?*, was the thought that began streaming in. After putting everything on the backseat, I turned around, there was my husband, going on ten years.

"I'm not saying this is the end," I heard myself say. It was like I was outside of my body, watching someone else speak for me. "I need to see something, anything. I can't live like this anymore."

Looking back, I don't know how I left that day. It was like someone had their hand on my back gently pushing me out the door. A force greater than me was helping, there's not a doubt in my mind.

The two of us grew up together. We met just after my seventeenth birthday. Both born and bred in small town America; he was from Virginia and I from Illinois. For some reason, the youth groups we were a part of went to the same church camp on the same week in Georgia that year. We became pen pals mailing care packages across the country and spent hours on the phone learning about one another. As a romance between us grew we became a couple that frequently traveled the twelve hour drive back and forth to see each other. Our life together began as a road trip.

He was my high school sweetheart, prom date, and first real love. Five years after we met that day in Georgia he would become my husband, both of us the ripe age of twenty-two on our wedding day. We made multiple moves across the country during our marriage, but our final stop was Austin, Texas. It's where we made a life together.

It all began to change with a phone call.

"I'm almost home," I told my parents. I parked my car and took in a breeze through the window. "What's up?"

"Well, we have some news," dad said in a somber tone. Both of my parents were on the line. *This can't be good.* Dad had struggled with health problems for years, Crhones (an intestinal disease that ravaged his intestines) being the pinnacle of his battle. The dread that was my constant companion throughout his illness readily made an appearance.

"It's cancer," he said with a painful crack in his voice.

"It's cancer. It's cancer. It's cancer," echoed through me, reverberating on a never-ending loop in the silence that followed. It fell into a hollowness I had never experienced within myself, bouncing around with nowhere to land. I don't recall anything else from our conversation except mom's offer for my sister and I to come home for a few days.

A quick flight to St. Louis, Missouri, we arrived at their house in Southern Illinois the following morning and spent the day digesting the news. Our family had some underlying issues that went deep; some grievances so securely rooted I didn't know if they would ever be resolved. Once the cancer discovery was made, everyone's perspectives began to radically shift, almost overnight. Holding so tightly to "rightness" didn't seem important anymore and the hard walls that had developed between us began to dissolve. It took a little humility, some big apologies on both sides, and unfortunately something life-threatening to turn it around.

Dad wasn't given much time initally, which threw everyone's lives into the air. One of the most turbulent encounters was for my foster sister who had come to stay with my parents. She had to leave us during this time, making the trauma expand. Her swift departure left a giant hole in our family, a wound without a remedy.

Not knowing how much time we would have with him, I stayed. I wanted to be there to help with drives to the hospital, provide emotional support, and assist mom with all the care he would require. He gave so much to me my entire life; there was nowhere else I'd rather be.

An unexpected health crisis didn't fit into the plan my husband and I had for ourselves, but moving home was a sacrifice I wanted to make. Always having made major decisions like that together, this was the first one I made on my own; one he didn't quite understand. In an effort to support me, he moved up a couple of months later with my sister and her husband after the birth of their first baby, my parents' first grandchild.

With everyone rallying around him, the days that followed are familiar to anyone who has had a brush with the disease. We were in a haunting new land the first several weeks. The grim scent of the sterile treatment center greeted us upon entering, lingering down the floorboards of hallways in a low fog. I had never felt fear in such a physically present way until the day of his first appointment; every cell in my body rigid. Rows and rows of families sat in the seven floors of waiting rooms, my mind naturally pinpointing the sick one of each grouping. There was no mistaking that look. They were slender ghostly figures who seemed as though they would shatter if you breathed the wrong way on an elevator. But after a while, it was normal. Our family had one, too.

We all became permanent fixtures at the hospital; we did puzzles in the lobby together, got used to coffee from a vending machine, kept dad company in chemo pods, packed picnic lunches, and befriended patients and staff. It was a rollercoaster of emergency procedures, surgeries, frequent hospital stays, some good news, and far more bad news. We became a united front and faced every turn and crossroads together, but dad wasn't himself, none of us were. It was a time full of upheaval for the whole family. We tried to lend extra patience to each other as we waded through the roughest waters we had ever faced, but our fuses often ran short. One small spark in conversation could send all of us into a full on manic wildfire in seconds. "Cancer changed everything" is not just a saying, it's the truth.

One of the biggest changes in my life was my relationship with my husband. The trials our family was experiencing left me with little energy to smooth things over with him, as I had always previously done. Over the years we had gradually fallen into a colorful array of destructive patterns; addiction, codependency, and abuse in its various forms. They didn't take hold overnight; we assumed our roles in this drama slowly, over time. I carried us for a lot of years, shouldering the majority of our responsibilities, but couldn't muster the resolve to blaze the trail any farther. When times got the toughest, he was no longer around. Not only was I going through a major transition with my dad, I didn't have my best friend backing me through it.

For years all of my time went into keeping our marriage together, or at least appearances. An overwhelming sense of helplessness began to fill me as I watched everything I built for myself unravel. I found my value in being a wife and homemaker and lost my sense of purpose when we separated. Layer by layer, my biggest support system was falling away.

We didn't speak until we met for dinner a few weeks into our separation. As I looked at him across that booth at a local restaurant it was like he was a stranger I had never met before. Like we were on a bizarre time warp of a blind date. The second time we met to go to marriage counseling. Our one and only session, and I was just as confused afterward as before.

I only went back to our home once to collect the last of my things. As I pulled up in the driveway we used to arrive in together, I could see the shadows of our former selves dance before me. A sharp pain formed behind my eyes as I watched us drift apart in slow motion. I looked through the cabinets of dishes and pans, counter with appliances, the closet of clothes, a fridge of leftovers, and decor we picked out together; the collection of things from our combined life.

"*Is this real?*" the thought so overpowering, surely I must have whispered it. It was too painful to take those things and use them in a life without my life partner. I didn't want to keep a thing.

As a girl, I envisioned myself being married to one person forever and always. One day we'd be that old retired couple on the front porch talking about all our years together, sitting around holiday dinner tables full of kids and grandkids, and the last ones on the floor during anniversary dances at weddings. All my hopes were riding on that idyllic picture for us, and I put every effort into keeping the dream alive. My whole world fell apart when the possibility of that life was no longer a reality.

Since we were so young when we met, he felt like my one shot at love. I had never been with anyone else and was raised to believe there was one man out there for me, my one fish in the sea. I had been hardwired for longterm rocksteady commitment. My parents and grandparents modeled that kind of marriage. It was in my blood. The "true love waits" ring I had around my left ring finger as a teenager before we got together was proof enough.

When I married him I vowed in my heart that divorce was not an option. I chose him and only him that day, and every day after. We had to hit the threshold of absolute chaos before the thought of leaving even entered my mind.

Once I left I discovered I didn't know who I was without him. Over the course of fifteen years I became a master chameleon; twisting and contorting into who I thought he wanted me to be. I listened to what he listened to, hung out where he hung out, ate what he ate, and talked about what he talked about. I suppose some of that blurring happens when you've been with someone for so long, but I could no longer recognize myself. Who was I? What did I want? I knew I didn't want to be his lookalike anymore. I wanted to be me.

One of my closest friends had just bought her first home and she graciously made one of her bedrooms available to me while I got on my feet. She provided a safe place to wander the new single road I found myself on and brought new people into my life when her friends visited, we watched movies together, and she surprised me with fun gifts like cupcakes to lift my spirits. A lot of my time was spent holed up in my room, bawling my eyes out as I watched reruns of old sitcoms I had seen a hundred times before. Everything felt strange; sleeping alone after sharing a bed for so long, meals by myself, and no companion to talk to.

The initial months apart were hard. I was quietly settling into a bottomless pool. With my face pointed toward the sky, I could feel the water lightly kiss my hairline and chin. Eyes closed, I could have floated and bobbed there forever never feeling, hearing, or saying anything again. I could still breathe, but just barely. It was calmer there. With my ears below the surface, I could block out the noise.

My search for healing began with a yoga class that met in an art gallery. Each wall was curated with care, the music selections were soothing, and the room was lit by candlelight. Even though many of the movements were new, my body folded naturally into them. The instructor would walk around to put hot cloths across our eyes as we laid in savasana, a gentle healing touch. With each restorative and strengthening pose I began the journey back to myself.

I didn't buy groceries for at least a month. A simple household chore, sure, but what was I supposed to buy for myself? My usual list consisted of everything he enjoyed. I didn't even know what I liked anymore, and I'd rather starve than have to face another challenge.

"Hey, I'm coming by to pick you up. We're going grocery shopping," my sister announced when she called one morning. As I tried to think of an excuse to get out of it she added, "And I know you don't have anything else going on, so we'll see you in a few."

I mumbled as I got ready, mumbled as I locked the door, and mumbled as I walked to her car. We arrived only to look in the backseat to see that her son had fallen asleep on the drive over. Usually we would sit in the car to let him nap, but this day was different. Our eyes connected—she was determined to see this mission through.

"I can carry him," I found myself offering. I wrapped his tiny arms around my neck, legs around my waist and put his head on my shoulder. She bundled her newborn in a carrier and we were off.

I tensed up as the glass doors automatically opened for us. The chilled draft of the AC as it merged with the air outdoors was jarring, throwing off my balance. I looked down at my nephew to center myself. *We were in the store.* This may seem like a small thing, but it was a HUGE (yes in all caps) accomplishment for me. My sister lovingly took my list, which probably had all of three items on it, and threw them and more into the cart.

"I've got it," she told me as she offered to pay for everything.

Normally one to object to help, she taught me to simply receive as I began to cry in the checkout line. She had become a pillar of stability in my otherwise tornado-wrecked-mess of a life. When I was completely depleted, she took care of me. Her husband and babies too. There's no way I would have made it through that experience without her and the embrace my nephew was wrapping me up in. He hugged me through the entire store.

The last time I'd see my ex was for a hike. It was my idea, thinking it could be a time where we'd discuss what our next steps would be since our future was still undecided. I was hoping with everything in me that he would give me a reason to stay. It felt easier to hang onto "us" and all of our broken parts rather than venture into entirely new terrain. Shortly into our ascent, through the few words we shared, I knew it was over. Staring at the dry cracked rocks beneath me, I felt myself crumble into them. The air collapsed around me. I would be filing for a divorce.

I spun out for a while. I was angry, reckless, and wrestled with thoughts like, *Why did I ever get married in the first place!? I wish I never met him, I could've been saved all this heartache!* I talked it over with a group of girlfriends I was out with one day.

"I would've never met you if it hadn't been for him," one of them replied.

Another chimed in saying the same thing, "Yeah, we met through our guys."

I looked around at that group of women and realized, I wouldn't have known any of them if it weren't for my time with him. During those first months my friends were present in ways I didn't know I needed. They actively listened as I most likely repeated stories about him, held space for me as I cried, made me dinner, and let me stay the night. All of this and more went through my head thinking of specific things each one had done to show me she cared. They threw the lifelines that brought me back.

Maybe our marriage didn't last forever, and that was sad, but I gained so much during my time with him. I would be forever thankful for where I came from, if not simply for those friends I was enjoying the company of that afternoon. I could choose to see my marriage through more than the lens of pain. I could be grateful for it.

No, it didn't work out, even blew up at the end. Was it worth it? Yes, and yes again. He was worth it. Our life together was worth it. Who I was becoming because of it was worth it. Perhaps one day, I would even become empowered by it.

Rather than wallowing in everything I didn't have anymore, which had become commonplace, I decided to think about what I still did have:

— me
— some stuff
— a car
— family and friends

As I saw it, there were two options: rent a place and find a job (the usual, which I had done my entire adult life) or try to think a bit more outside the box. With my tax return in view, which provided the funding initially, I decided to utilize the resources I had and began to plan my first solo road trip across the United States. Gas was cheap, my expenses were at an all-time low, and I'd get the opportunity to reconnect with friends I hadn't seen in ages. A lot had changed during our years apart; marriages, children, new homes... on and on the list went. As is the nature with young families, we gradually became isolated from one another, each busy building our own tiny empire.

Having no outstanding bills, kids of my own, or household to maintain I had nothing to lose, so I packed everything I owned into my hatchback and hit the road. Both terrified and excited, I took a giant leap into the unknown. I visited friends I grew up with that had since moved away, went back to places I used to live, stayed with extended family members, and stopped in to see friends from college. Since I wasn't sure who I was anymore, I wanted to explore who they were. Perhaps since they were part of my past, I could find my future in them as well. Surely a piece of them was a piece of me.

I was adrift in the early days of my trip. A map told me where to go, outlining the journey ahead, but my life was the stark opposite; feeling murky, unclear, and out of my control for the very first time. I didn't know what was coming around the next bend, what I was doing, or how I was going to make it. On I-70 heading eastbound my first trip, *"Love is worth it,"* was written in large red spray painted letters on the side of an overpass. I'd find love again. I knew it was still out there.

On a visit to Oklahoma to see one of my closest friends from childhood, the tears began to roll as I told her how I felt like a failure in comparison. Her life was the story we played with our dolls when we were young. A loving husband, two children, great job, and a gorgeous home; the whole American Dream package.

"What happened to me!?" I lamented. "I'm out wandering around the country, living out of my car, no husband, kids, home, or job!" She put her hand on my arm, beginning to tear up, too.

"Don't you know? I feel the same way about you. You get to travel and see things I don't know if I ever will," she replied. That night we took down the fence between us once we realized the grass was green on both sides of it. One lawn manicured and the other overgrown, our lives were equally beautiful in different ways.

I also visited a woman who had become a second mom to me, my mother-in-law, and the rest of the family in Virginia. I loved her like my own mother, still did even though my relationship with her oldest son had changed. She was my "mama" and I was her "baby girl" for fifteen years. Losing my husband was hard enough; I was afraid I'd also be losing his family. I grew up with them, known them half of my life. They had become *my* family.

"Virginia is for Lovers," read the welcome sign as I crossed the state line. I wondered if it could be for more than just lovers. It had been my stomping grounds for so long. Would there still be a place for me?

My fears were relieved upon my arrival; Mama had planned an entire day with me. We met for breakfast at one of our favorite local greasy spoons, saw a movie at the theater, stopped by grandma's house to give her hugs and say hello, then went back to their family home for dinner.

I got choked up as we walked through the front door; all of her pictures were still up. There was a shelf with photos of my ex and I from prom and a formal from college, a photo on the refrigerator from a holiday card we sent out one year, our wedding photos, and other framed snapshots were throughout their home. It was virtually a time capsule of our love and life together.

We shook off the feelings with my niece's in an impromptu dance party in the kitchen. They gave me a makeover, we played boardgames, and all of us sat around the dinner table laughing and sharing stories like always. While not the same as it used to be (it was my first visit to his parents' house without him) they made it clear that they still loved me.

While I was housesitting for a friend in Ohio, it dawned on me that I stepped into her life for the week. I fed her animals, tended and watered her garden, made food in her kitchen, and the arms of her couch held me as I slept during my stay. After a long day of caring for her home, I sat in front of her wood stove with her dogs and kitty snuggled around me. As I looked out her large window stargazing, I thought of all the lives that were a part of my trip, amazed by the trust I was given from my friends.

An army of strong women surrounded, supported, and pushed me on throughout my journey, my sacred feminine tribe. Whether it was a gathering of friends like the annual girls night I looked forward to each year in my hometown, or an individual visit, they opened their hearts and homes across the country, giving me the opportunity to observe and sample different approaches to life. I helped with DIY projects, made meals, attended children's choir performances and dance recitals, talked through job stresses and relationship woes, held garage sales, dealt with car problems, and helped their kids with homework and read them books before bed.

Some of the more colorful firsts I was introduced to were a day of doggie daycare in Maine, the Women's March and a monster truck rally in Washington D.C., a holiday lights tour of New Orleans, a princess lunch at Walt Disney World, my first concert at Madison Square Garden in New York City, behind the scenes at Baseball Spring Training and a trip to a shooting range in Florida, a Blue Angels flight demonstration in Virginia, a drag show in Minneapolis, the Grand Ole Opry in Nashville, and a motorcycle ride up the eastern coast of Lake Michigan.

A white 2010 Toyota Prius, that was originally my dad's, was my getaway car across the country. He gave it to me when he became too weak to drive. Later a friend named her Maude, which means "powerful battler," and she was. She powered through extreme weather, some unbelievable roads, and saw me through my internal battle the whole way.

I learned how to take care of her so she could keep me moving forward, whether it was adding oil (because she burned through it like a fiend on hills), figuring out how to put new wipers on in the parking lot of an auto supply store, or taking a break to let her cool down for a bit. I'm reminded of a time when I sat by the road in the desert while waiting to add coolant, steam rising from under her hood.

She became my friend. Wacko as it sounds, I talked to her. Putting my hand on the dash after a fun winding road I'd tell her, "Whoa, that was stellar! You handled that so well!" Or after a serious pothole, "My bad!" I became a crazy cat lady, only with a car.

I laid the seats flat to camp in her countless times and slept in the drivers seat at truck stops, rest areas, and parking lots. Maude was not only my car; she became my bedroom, kitchen, living room, laundry room, porch, reading nook, and bathroom (only when I was desperate)! She was my home. We had dance parties, lifted weights, sang, ate, slept, read, listened to audiobooks and podcasts, and shared conversations with God and the Universe.

She was my time machine, and the freeways across America were my way of teleporting to another place. I was both pilot and copilot, and learned to navigate solo like a pro. I figured out road signs, how to read maps, and calculated when to stop for gas with mile markers. Soon I began connecting the space between people and towns within me. Even though they had different lives, I found that someone in Kansas could be very similar to someone in Vermont.

One of the greatest gifts I received on my journey was meeting six women who became my sisters. We worked together in Santa Fe, New Mexico for a summer and shared an instantaneous connection. It's like the clouds parted and the heavens handed me exactly who I needed right when I needed them.

What would have been my ten-year wedding anniversary fell right in the middle of our summer together. After my wedding day, my mom sent my dress to a company that vacuum sealed it in a box so it wouldn't yellow or fade over time. "Your love preserved forever," it read upon opening. I had looked at that box in a closet at my parents house for months, usually bursting into tears each time I saw it. The day I packed my car to leave for New Mexico I thought of that box in the closet and ran back in to get it. As I shoved it into the trunk of the car my mother's knowing eyes fixed on me.

"It'll be okay, mom. I'll be okay," I said somewhat flippantly, trying not to cry. We both began to weep as she wrapped her arms around me. Like a sheltering tree, she had always tried to protect me from getting hurt.

My new friends and I decided to make a photography project out of the dress. Being a photographer, it was new for me to be the subject in front of a camera, but I put all of my feelings into their images. I had never been to that part of the country before and found the dry landscape rejuvenating. We took the dress to locations all across the state where I swam in lakes wearing it, climbed between rocks, and even posed nude. *I was fearless!* It became a way of releasing my pain and provided a way to explore what life would look like without him.

We ended the summer with a camping excursion to Santa Fe National Forest. The seven of us collected outdoor gear, champagne, and candy then drove deep into the woods. They wrote "Just Divorced" across the back windows of the two cars we piled into, so folks honked and congratulated me the entire drive. The purpose of our trip: burn the dress.

I sat a while looking at the delicate blue beadwork I lovingly embroidered on it for our special day. More than anything I wanted a blue and white dress. Since I couldn't find one, I added an intricate pattern of beading myself. Then I flipped it over to see the remnants of our project where I waded through mud, painted it in bright colors, it was torn, and there were grass stains everywhere. It was completely destroyed. I wailed over my dress like I didn't know I could.

"*My love! My marriage! My life!*" I cried.

Once the tears subsided, I became quiet and looked at it again. The pristine side was perfect, exactly how I planned for it to be. The other side was messy and wild, yet mysteriously elegant in a new way. My old and new lives were brought together in that one garment.

Everyone stood back as I held it up like it was standing over the fire. The flames crept their way up the fabric and it started to morph and melt like plastic. From white, yellow, brown, to black; it began to disappear. With a whoosh a dark smoke cloud rose to touch the treetops as it hit the ground, letting off a horrid smell as all the toxins from my life with him burned away. My friends encircled me, sang to me, and held my hands; completely and wholly present. The best friends a girl could ask for. When we were ready to turn in for the night one of our camping experts doused it with water.

We all crammed into three small tents positioned in a triangle, their zipper doors facing each other. As I drifted off to sleep I thought of each of my friends there with me, their faces entering my consciousness one by one. I was grateful to them and for them. That summer they helped me find an ending to my marred love story so I could pick up the pieces and begin again. I could still have a happily ever after, even though my life would be going in a drastically different direction than expected.

The next morning I was the first one awake. As I got out of the tent I caught a glimmer out of the corner of my eye. I walked over to the circle of stones from our campfire. A portion of the dress didn't burn! Blackened around the edges, there was a piece of my dress staring back at me. I kept it for almost a year, safe in a shoebox wrapped in multi-colored tissue paper. When I came across it during a cleanse of my belongings, I was finally ready to throw the last piece away. Like everything else, discarding it was a process that took time.

A new friend I met the following week offered the next step on my healing quest when she offered me a set of mala beads (something I had never heard of before). She had just completed a 40-day cleanse with them and suggested that perhaps I was ready to start my own, teaching me how to meditate, chant, and sing with them—a practice that would help me through some of the toughest things I would face. I made the practice my own, sometimes counting them like sheep to usher in sleep, or extending my gratitude practice by saying something I was grateful for with each one, or my favorite and most challenging, praying specifically for a friend with each one. Coming up with something to say about 108 people is a lot!

I wanted to make a trip out to California after my time in the southwest. It seemed like a good idea. I had never been on my solo venture and was looking for a fresh start. A part of me also wanted to run away. That day I packed my dress into the car, my dad stood alongside my mom. He looked frail. I had already talked with him about turning down the job. I didn't want to leave if his health was going to take a turn for the worse, but he wanted me to go. He knew it would be a great opportunity.

"I'll be here when you get back," his voice sang back in promise, even though he looked worried.

Towards the end of the summer I received calls from both my mom and sister delivering the same warning: "Dad's not doing so well. I think you should come home," they said. The underlying urgency in these calls had become a regular occurrence, but this time was different. Dad called too.

"I think you should probably come home," he said, his voice low and scratchy.

My heart sank. I had put my best efforts into denial, thinking it would push back the inevitable or at least I wouldn't have to face it. Having far outlived any life expectancy predictions, now almost three years in after an initial diagnosis of stage four colon cancer, to me, he was superhuman! Even cancer couldn't phase him! Normally the one to say, "Oh, I'll be fine girls!" a new truth was surfacing.

"Do you think you'll be stopping through Texas on your way back?" he added.

"I hadn't planned on it. It's not exactly on the way," I managed to stutter. I was stunned, knowing exactly what he was implying.

"Well maybe… think about finishing the thing," he said cryptically with the aid of several long pauses.

After attempting to gulp the air like a fish out of water, I asked, "Would that give you some kind of peace, Dad?"

"Yes," he replied. "But don't do it for me or anybody else. Do it for yourself and only if you're ready."

What he was saying under his words was that he was concerned about my safety and wellbeing. That if, heaven forbid, something were to happen to him, he wanted to protect me even if that meant postmortem. He was hoping I would stop through Austin to finalize my divorce. I had filed there months before and planned to return at some point that year to complete it. Perhaps if it would give him some peace, it could do the same for me.

At the added encouragement of the family I was staying with and a few friends through work who had lost a parent, I decided to make the trek back to the heart of the country, first stopping through the Capital of Texas on the way to finalize my divorce. The lengths I had come with the help of my friends that summer gave me the courage to finish it.

After meeting with multiple lawyers and signing a stack of papers, I had a few hours over lunchtime to kill but didn't want to wait in that stale cold building. I needed fresh air and my meter was about to run out anyway. I hopped in the car with no destination in mind. *"My spot,"* I thought.

I have a favorite place to sit in the middle of Zilker Park in Austin, known to some as Rock Island. It's a huge group of rocks at the center of a large grassy area. Collectively, I've spent many hours lying there reading and looking up at the clouds. There's an amazing view of the city and it's great for people watching. Dogs run around after frisbees, young athletic types play volleyball on sand-filled courts and pick up games of football on the lawn, and others like me are just doing their own thing. Kids often climbed around me as I sat, the rock somewhat of a jungle gym to them. I enjoyed the company and busyness around me. I could quiet it all in my mind.

I stopped through the last place my ex and I ate together on the way and picked up a veggie burger, fries, and a strawberry shake; comfort foods. The overcast skies made the park quiet that day. As usual, no one was sitting in my chosen alcove, so I spread out my picnic to enjoy my last few hours as a wife.

My thoughts transported me through the highlights of all our years together. A reel that, even on that day, made me long for that normal again. Then the low points began to play; all of the reasons I had to gather the strength to leave him. The fog of thoughts lifted as a woman with a camera asked if she was in my way. I was in my own little world and hadn't even noticed other people around.

"I'm sorry," she said again. "Do you mind if we take a few quick shots? It's such a great view of the city from up here!" An engagement photo session. A couple blinked eagerly at me as they held onto each other behind her.

"Not at all. Go for it," I replied as I looked up at the sky. *"Really?"* I silently asked.

They crowded in next to me to get the one other spot with a view of the city. They were so close it was impossible not to overhear them. They were given prompts like, "Will you put your arm around her? Make sure I can see the ring. Look into each others eyes. Go ahead, kiss her!" The couple laughed as one always feels awkward when given this set of directions. We felt the same way when a friend took our engagement photos. That momentary discomfort fades when you look into the eyes of someone you love. It becomes something funny that makes you laugh, which in the end makes for great pictures.

I felt blank as I drove back to the courthouse; the absolute last place I wanted to be. My tummy gurgled and turned, not from the food, because of nerves. My body pleaded with me to run in any direction but the one I was headed.

I sat in a courtroom surrounded by strangers and waited to be called, staring at my wedding ring that I had put on the opposite hand. I moved my fingers back and forth slightly, watching it sparkle in the sunshine coming in through the window. It threw me back in time to when I first received it, as I watched it make rainbows across the ceiling.

He proposed in the same place where we had our first dance. He knelt down on one knee holding a small white box that matched the snow on the ground around him. Those five diamonds (one for each year we had been together) shone like stars in the inky night. Wearing it was my way of connecting with him that day. Our last day together even though I was finishing it alone.

Another woman was summoned before me who was doing the same thing. She was given a form to read which outlined how she was unable to reconcile her marriage including a detailed account of their time together; children or no children, assets to split, how long the separation had been, and the like. She spoke so quickly I barely caught it. I'm sure she was trying to get through it as fast as possible without crying. I began to tear up sensing the feelings she was bottling in her voice.

Then I was called out to the hallway by a lawyer who informed me how everything would go down. I let him know I didn't think I could read that document. I was blubbering uncontrollably already. I don't know if he even understood me. He said he would speak with the judge and excused me to the restroom to freshen up. Upon reentering the courtroom, the place had filled up, so I sat in the back.

While I waited I had the strangest vision. The courtroom looked like a church with rows of wooden pews and an aisle down the middle. I would be walking down it to stand in front of an authority to reverse the first time I walked down the aisle. When called, "*Miss* (insert married name here)" for the first time in my life, I rose, held my papers in my hands like a bouquet, and cried down the aisle like I did on our wedding day. This time they weren't tears of joy.

As I approached the bench the judge scooted a tissue box out to me. Unlike with the woman who did this before, he spoke very quietly.

"This is just between you and me," he said. "I'm sorry this is such a hard day."

I relaxed and nodded using a tissue to wipe away the tears. Instead of having me read through the form, he read it, asking me to simply respond "yes" or "no" where appropriate. We spoke in hushed tones through what sounded like a two-part poetry reading. Once we made it through, the room finally stopped spinning.

"Now I'm going to add my signature to the two of yours and that makes this final, okay?" he said. And that was it. I walked out of that courtroom a new woman. I was finally "officially" free.

After the fact, many people have told me something along the lines of, "Thankfully that chapter in your life is over. You can put that book up on a shelf." But it was more like the book was shredded and I was standing in a pile of its torn pages, dust and debris littering the floor around me, mayhem still fresh in the air. *What happened to my life? Better yet, what am I supposed to do now?*

I didn't know if I would ever be able to pick up the pieces. I thought I'd never get through it, never move on. Life was o-v-e-r. But it wasn't. Life was just beginning.

poppy's the moon

It felt like I lived my entire life over again that month. After finalizing my divorce, I got in my car and drove straight from Texas to Illinois to see my dad. He collapsed into our hug on the driveway when I pulled up as if to say, "I can finally rest." He had been waiting for me.

"I told you I'd be here when you got back," he said weakly in a voice I hardly recognized. I shared panicked glances with my mom as I hugged him, seeing the now grapefruit-sized tumors growing around his neck.

"Why didn't you guys tell me!?" I exclaimed.

"We didn't want to worry you, honey," she replied in full cry.

He went into the hospital on a Tuesday a couple of days after I got back. He had mowed the lawn the previous week, grilled a barbecue feast for a group of our family and friends to celebrate my return that weekend, and even went to work that morning... *slam*. He was put in a room on the seventeenth floor, or "the penthouse" as he called it, always finding that silver lining.

One night, mom decided to stay with him so I left bound for their house knowing I'd take the next shift. Over the years we routinely switched back and forth staying nights while he was in the hospital. It was comforting for him to have one of us there; a piece of home.

When I got to the car I wasn't ready to go back to their house all alone and the thought of a former coworker who's dad had passed away suddenly the year before came to mind. The whole time we worked together we prepared for it to be my dad, given his diagnosis. It was a total shock when her dad was first. I was already on her radar. She knew I was spending nights at the hospital and checked in with me regularly to see how I was doing. Since her own father wrestled with a longterm health condition, she knew what it was like and was a great friend to me during that tumultuous time.

We met up at a bar with a rousing installment of 90's trivia going on that we would've normally jumped in on, but everything fell into background noise as we talked about our dads. It helped so much to hear her story, her dad's story, and her family's story.

"What are we going to do if something happens to him?" I asked her.

She told me her relationship with her father didn't end when he died. Somehow, it carried on in a new way. As she spoke I recalled seeing her family lined up in front of the church during his visitation. She wore a black tea-length dress with a large floral print across it; so lovely for her daddy. As friends greeted her family offering their condolences, fear dropped deep in my stomach. When I went through the line to hug her, I imagined she was passing the baton to me.

"I still talk to my dad and feel him with me all the time," she said with certainty.

As I looked at her, I saw how resilient she had become. Would I ever be that strong? When we walked out to the parking lot she held me in a true heart hug before we parted. As a daughter with a shared experience, I felt her give a portion of her strength to me. Once I made it back to my parents house that night, I was able to ease into a few hours of sleep. She calmed something in me.

Dad was nearing the end of his battle with cancer, and we were told as much at the hospital the next day. When asked "what he wanted to do?" by doctors, he took a deep breath in and out, eyes wide at the floor. He looked up slowly, a tear glistening in the corner of his right eye.

"I don't want to die here," he managed to say as a look I had never seen on him before presented itself—fear.

There would be no more calls to doctors or emergency visits to the hospital. We were moving into the unchartered waters of hospice care at home. As we loaded him and his oxygen tank into the car I realized… we were going to have to watch this happen.

Family and friends flew to our rescue from across the country wanting to help. Everyone buzzed around the house in a flurry trying to keep him comfortable. I was immobile, numb, unable to function or process the turn of events that had happened within a matter of days. *Wait, I'm divorced and my dad's on hospice!? How did this happen so fast?*

Each family member and friend who sacrificed their own schedules to be there provided mountains of support when we needed them most. I wouldn't have made it through those initial days without them. They had all come to spend time with dad in case it was their last opportunity;

another facet of realism beginning to sink in. Once the out-of-towners prepared to head back to their corners of the country, I stepped into the role before me and decided to be thankful, glad even, that I could care for and serve him in that way.

We didn't have many visitors as dad had requested this. The space around him was reserved for only the closest of family and friends. Like his business partner of thirty years, his financial advisor who he entrusted his livelihood with, and friends from church who were like brothers to him. They each had the ability to make him laugh and brought great joy to all of us as they reflected on everything they had been through together. There were lifelong friends who flew across the country just to make us a meal and mop the kitchen floor (mom's least favorite of chores and one which dad had always done), couple friends that my parents spent many evenings enjoying the company of over the years brought gifts and held space for them to speak their feelings about the whole ordeal, and his assistants from work came to remove stitches from past surgeries and check on his various skin conditions.

Aside from these occasional visits, every day was a family day. We spent afternoons sitting on the back porch laughing and talking about all our years together. He loved being outside. Even when it was a struggle to get him there, we always tried to make a way. He'd lay his head back and close his eyes feeling the sun on his eyelids and soaking into his skin, taking it all in with a sigh; a brief moment of relief.

All of us read together in his bedroom while he faded in and out of sleep. Mom held my nephew as he drank his bottle, my sister nursed the baby next to her husband, the dog laid at dad's feet, and I took whatever space was left usually taking pictures. All of us in a tangle on the bed together.

"There's always something new to learn," he'd say.

Mom bought gymnastics mats, a playhouse, and a kitchen set for my sister's kids. Since dad was unable to go downstairs to their playroom and taking walks even with his wheelchair was becoming more of a challenge, we worked together to make the living room a fun place where he could play with his grandchildren. They were the lights of his life. The kids prepared pretend meals from their kitchen, took him to the land of make-believe, and played house together. We were all dad's caregivers, even them.

Throughout his years of illness, everything he loved and loved doing was slowly taken away from him. His body made simple things impossible. He was an active man all his life, a star on sports teams as a kid, he graduated to triathlons later in life. He learned that no matter how healthy he ate, self-driven he was, or how many hours he put in at the gym, cancer held no prejudice. It could happen to anyone.

The hardest and final of these losses would be his work. The forever student, he stretched himself always wanting to learn more; new tools, additional certifications, and conferences on difficult procedures. He was a dedicated Oral Surgeon and loved helping people. One day he scribbled some thoughts on paper, asked for the phone, and time by himself. I waited in the hallway in case he were to call for help. Finally getting a private moment, he began to cry softly. After giving him a few minutes I opened the door.

"Are you okay, Dad?" I asked.

He looked up at me as tears hit his knees. Sitting on the edge of the bed, he patted the spot next to him with his hand. An invitation to sit.

"You don't mind if I'm in here?" I asked.

He shook his head no, I closed the door behind me, and he began to dial a number he knew well; his office of nearly thirty years. His business partner had retired, so he asked by name for the doctor who bought their practice only months earlier. He waited silently and set his notes to the side. He didn't need them for this one.

"I wanted to call to let you know, I don't think I'll be able to come in anymore," he said.

He went quiet while he listened. Reassuring words on the other end made his face beam for a moment, his voice shaking as he got off the phone. Then, with the push of a button, the hardest call he ever had to make was over. Such a brief conversation for one of the biggest turning points in a man's life. He was finally admitting that he would never be returning to work, or normal life, again.

As he hung up he let out the rush of emotion he was holding in, an inner howl. I had never seen him cry like that before. Everything that brought him joy in this world, apart from our family, was taken from him. His childlike body crumpled into mine, utterly defeated. I propped him up with a few pillows and ran down the hall to get mom, who had just stepped out of her first shower in days. Hair still dripping, she threw a towel around her body and ran down the hall to him.

"What's the matter!?" she asked frantically. He didn't answer, head hanging with his back arched low as tears streamed down his cheeks.

"He just called the office," I answered.

She rolled his wheelchair over to the edge of the bed, sat on it in front of him, and he lowered his head into her hands. As I closed the door, I glanced into the room, the light filtering in through the sheer curtains behind them. As they sat there in close embrace crying together, I knew that moment would be eternally etched on my heart.

We threw a retirement party for him, even though he was forced with the decision. In an attempt to brighten the day we decorated the dining room with palm trees affixed to the curtains that my sister, brother-in-law, and I made out of poster board complete with papier-mâché coconuts, mom made him a coconut cake (one of his favorites), and the grandkids made art that we decorated the china cabinet and windows with. His family took him to the beach, his favorite place on earth, one more time. As he sat in his spot at the head of the table, oxygen tubing running across the room from a noisy machine affixed to his nose, he wept softly as he looked through cards, well wishes, and photographs from the staff at his office of all their years together—not a dry eye in the room.

At his sister's suggestion, I read scripture from Psalms aloud to him while he slept. She thought it would be a comforting sound. With a pillow at the foot of the bed laying opposite him, I was positioned to hold his hand. If he were to be startled awake, which happened often, I'd be there.

"I'm right here dad," I'd say as he smiled and went back to sleep.

I figured if it were me laying in that bed, I wouldn't want to wake up alone. Sometimes he'd relay his dreams about his mother who died when he was young, being outside in a large open space running through tall grasses, or about his grandchildren in the future. Once waking up in tears, saying how much he would miss them. He had a foot in two worlds, life and death; his dreams the space in-between.

He also had visions while he was awake. He saw two figures accompanying my sister into his room and also saw them pacing around the perimeter of the yard. She liked to think of them as angels guarding his spirit. He told us when the grandkids would run by he saw trails of color behind them; a visual of the energy in the air as they split through it.

"What color is it? Blue, red, green?" mom asked.

"It's not any of those colors," he replied. "It's just *color*."

This color was also on butterflies and dragonflies he'd see floating around the house, so we made finger-painted bugs and birds for him and taped them on lamps and other fixtures around the house. He saw lettered signs in the woods but grew frustrated when he couldn't quite make out what they said. The upper corners of the room started to curve around him like a cave, no longer able to see sharp corners. Once in a while he'd realize his visualizations were an illusion that only he could see, the logical side of his brain coming back momentarily.

"There's no one there is there?" he asked one time upon seeing someone sitting in an empty chair across the room. "I don't know what's worse, seeing something that's not there, or experiencing it alone," he said. I wanted so badly to see what he saw. His visions were fantastical, otherworldly.

I waited as long as I could to have one talk with him. I had been holding out hope that if we gave him good enough care we could steer him back to the path of wellness. When I finally accepted that saving him was beyond the bounds of possibility, I sobbed as I spoke with him about it.

"I'm starting this whole new life. What am I going to do without you? You've always been there to guide me. I need you now more than ever," I cried.

After a few minutes of silence he finally said, "Honey, you know what I'd say." So few words due to the effort they took to procure.

I awoke to him coughing one morning, sounding lighter and weaker that day. As I approached the room I could smell the peppermint and frankincense oils we used to relieve his sore muscles and moisturize his skin, then I heard mom humming to him as she bathed him in bed. The song was so familiar, like I remembered it from the womb. As I rounded the corner she welcomed me with a faint smile, her tired eyes brimming with tears as she gazed at me and then back to her love. He looked exhausted, as did she, as did I. None of us had been getting much sleep. The sun not even up yet, his needs seemed to exceed the hours in a day.

The three of us girls, my mom, sister, and I, bathed him, changed his clothing, cut his hair and nails, shaved his face, brushed his teeth, massaged his achy muscles, readjusted his positioning and straightened his bedding, did immeasurable loads of laundry since he was sweating through everything, washed dishes, managed and administered his medicine, ordered supplies, cleaned his ports and bandaged areas, fed him through a feeding tube that went through his abdomen, drained his lungs with a compression system from tubing that came out of his sides, helped him go to the bathroom, emptied his ostomy bag since his colon had been removed, and worked with hospice staff when they came. Time had become a dizzying blur. We were all in a fight for his survival, as well as our own. There was never a moment where there wasn't something to be done.

How long are we going to be able to do this? we each wondered in silence.

All of us took turns watching the kids, shifting roles so that my sister could have time with him. With two under the age of three, her husband shouldered a lot of their care, understanding how precious each minute we had with him was.

Dad was distraught searching for his mother, who had long been disceased, in the days before, once shouting, *"Mom, I can't find you!"* This day, while their Pastor, who was like a son to him, held his hand in prayer, he stretched out his arms as he looked upwards and called out, *"MOM!"*

As he spoke his face softened peacefully like he saw her right in front of him. He was going to be with her soon. I can only imagine she was holding her arms open the same way, having waited so long to hold her baby again.

Even though his physical form was changing I could still see the man I always knew and loved. I could see him practicing on softball fields and sledding with my sister and I when we were young; him being the biggest kid at the park, putting his arm around mom as they sat in church or talking with her out on the patio, and rolling the grandkids around in his wheelbarrow and taking them for rides on his lawnmower. I could hear his thunderous laugh, the one that unashamedly exploded through the air when something caught him just right, clear as a bell, even though he was virtually motionless.

Throughout the day a disturbing grimace built across his face, his body wrenched in ways that didn't seem physically possible, and his breathing became unbearably labored. It was torture for him, and for us to watch. Nothing soothed him—not water, morphine, or anything else. His spirit was outgrowing the dwelling it was given. It wouldn't be able to hold him much longer.

Later that day he woke up while I was reading to him. He shifted his head slightly to look at me.

"I sure do love you, Rachie," he said.

A phrase I heard from him throughout my life more times than I can count. It was his rule never to leave home without telling family how much they mean to you. This originated from a regret of not saying those words before his mother's unexpected passing. They would be his final words to me.

"I love you too, Dad," I replied.

That afternoon mom came in to give him a kiss but he gave no response. Even when he could no longer get out of bed or talk much, he had always pursed his lips to meet hers. Something had changed. She cried, I cried.

We called for my sister and she and mom laid with him; talking, weeping, sleeping, and holding him close. As they did, I laid on the carpet just beyond the foot of the bed staring up at the ceiling fan, my understanding of what was happening looping upside-down continually in empty space the same way. That was the moment it became real for me. The pace of caring for him had slowed and I finally had a moment to take a breath and let the knowing sink deep into my bones. We were going to lose him, the only question was, *when?*

That evening my brother-in-law and I were in his room to keep him company. After turning off the hockey game, dad's favorite sport to watch and play, I pulled out a card game that a friend of ours made. My mom and sister came in to join us once the kids were in bed and the kitchen was put back together. We sat around dad laughing and learning about one another, even bringing him in on the game. When prompted to compliment each player, I told dad he was the bravest man I know and that we were thankful for everything he had done for us. I leaned over and kissed him on the temple, his skin warm and waxy. He gave no response, but I know he heard me.

All of us grew tired and decided to call it a night. We began to discuss our options for the evening hours, all wanting to be there if that was to be *the* night. We prayed together for guidance, each of us in our own way.

When we looked up at him afterwards it took our breath away. While we were praying his color had changed and breathing slowed. It was like he saw us playing that game, then praying for him, and knew we would take care of each other. He had done all he could for us. It was time.

Just then, we heard what sounded like a knock at the front door. My brother-in-law went to check on it and mom followed. No one was there. Later mom would say she thought it was Jesus knocking, coming to take him home.

My sister thought it would be nice if we sang to him while we waited, so we began softly singing hymns he liked. She picked up the harmonies and I the melody, our voices so similar they melted to one. Mom came back and sat at the side of the bed caressing his hand as we sang. His girls were singing him into glory.

There was a moment where his eyes changed; a spark left. He was looking at me when this happened. It felt like part of his spirit left him and entered me in that precise second, a profound and startling transference of energy. Feeling a little rattled but serene, I looked down and noticed that I could no longer see his chest rise and fall.

"Girls, I think he stopped breathing," my voice slowing, hardly able to give life to the words.

My sister checked his pulse at his neck, then his wrist.

"I can't tell if I'm feeling my pulse or his," she questioned.

As she got up to get her husband for help, the baby monitor lit up. Her daughter's high pitched cries shrieked through the speaker, its light going into the deepest shade of red. For a moment I thought it was me, my inner child crying out for my daddy, *"No! Please, don't go!"* Their son, a fairly sound sleeper, also awoke, like they knew he was leaving us.

"Look!" mom exclaimed, as my sister, her husband, and their baby girl came back into the room.

A huge gust of wind came in the open window. I left one open, once hearing that it provides an easier way for a spirit to leave a dwelling. The curtain billowed into the room like a sail on a boat and air swirled around the room making it windy and cool. We were all transported out to sea, the room becoming our ship through the dark and dreary night. An overwhelming presence was all around us. We stood in absolute awe.

My niece lifted her arm toward the ceiling, looking upwards, pointing directly above us. "Do you think she can see something?" my brother-in-law asked tearfully.

She lowered her arm to touch his and stroked it gently to comfort him. As my sister began to cry she did the same to her leg. Their daughter wasn't even a year old yet, but she could sense the energy around her. Perhaps being the closest to the other side of life, the beginning, she knew best what was happening.

A heavy rest came over me as I laid in my usual position with my head at the foot of the bed, and while holding dad's hand, I fell into a deep sleep. When I awoke he was as pale as the linens enveloping him and his grip on my hand had tightened. He seemed to lose half of his body mass in the time I was asleep, like when all the air is sucked out of a balloon, his kind face now hollow. I pried my hand out of his, even though I never wanted to let go. His life, the true being he is, was not there anymore.

Needing some fresh air, my sister and her husband stepped outside. They stood in the driveway and looked up at the sky, each of their senses hyperaware after what we had just experienced. There were large white clouds rolling away from the house that they imagined to be grand horses carrying his spirit away. The moon and stars shown brilliantly, there was a heightened smell of the forest after a light rain, and the sounds of owls calling and insects chirping reminded them that dad was everywhere. He's all around us now, in nature.

Eventually the doorbell rang and we opened the door to two men outfitted in their Sunday best; black suits, ties, and shiny shoes. Something dad would have worn to service on Christmas. Our family knew both of them well. One was dad's friend, they used to meet for a men's prayer breakfast together, and the other was the older brother of one of my best friends from high school. I was thankful we knew them. It was such a private moment for our family and they instilled an unexpected sense of peace in all of us. Since they had known dad in life we knew they would take excellent care of him in the moment of his passing as well. I ran into the bedroom to let dad know they were there.

"They'll take good care of you daddy," I said as I kissed his cheek, now ice cold.

Mom and I stayed in the room to watch as his body was moved.

"Normally folks don't stay around to watch this, but you're more than welcome to," they told us. I had to watch to know he was really gone. It was a quiet, sacred ritual.

My friend's brother took a sheet from a bag and, as if by magic, thrust it from its folded state to an expansive parachute above dad's body. It floated down through the air to cover him ever so gently. The air current it created grazed across the faces of my mother and I, moving delicately through our hair. I closed my eyes as his essence wafted around us for the very last time. One at his head, one at his feet, they moved him to a gurney. Then dad's friend presented a fluffy green and white quilt.

"We just took this out of the dryer so he'll be nice and warm," he said. Wrapped in the quilt, they brought him out to the living room where the rest of the family waited.

"Rest easy daddy," my sister said as she gave his forehead a kiss.

"I love you sweetheart," was mom's final goodbye, her tears falling on his cheeks as she kissed him.

When they moved to cover his face with the sheet and quilt, I almost objected, "But he…!" then held my tongue. *Oh yeah, he no longer needs air to breathe.*

In the same moment the dog leapt from her resting spot on dad's rocking chair across the room surprising all of us, like he was getting up to leave. She had a sweet attentive way of caring for him, sensing he wasn't feeling well and hanging close to his side that month. She wanted to say goodbye too. As my brother-in-law picked her up they rolled him out the front door and down the sidewalk that led up to their house as mom walked silently behind them. The rest of us watched from the entranceway until we could no longer see him.

After everyone had gone to bed I walked through the house and turned off the lights that went on throughout the night. It had been an incredibly long day, yet I wasn't tired at all. I could have stayed up all night, but mom asked if I'd sleep next to her. She couldn't sleep by herself after he was taken away. It would be her first night without him in forty years, her first night as a widow. This meant I would sleep where he passed away only hours earlier. When I reminded her of this later she apologized.

"Oh my! I didn't even think about that, I was so exhausted!" she said.

Her first night of uninterrupted sleep since he came home from the hospital a month before, she was out in minutes. I laid there looking at the shadows on the ceiling for what felt like hours replaying memories of dad through the years, wondering how he felt in his final hours lying there.

I thought about the introspective spiritual practice that we observed him go through as he prepared for the next life, which began the day he discovered he had a terminal disease. He had taught me to cherish the wonder in every moment and that each day is a miracle if I'll only see it that way. I knew he wouldn't want our family to hide away in a never-ending abyss after his passing. He'd want us to let light in again, and people, and live as fully as he did. In the end, he wasn't scared to leave this world. He believed that he was going to a better place. Even though he didn't want to go, he was ready.

No one knows exactly what happens after we take our last breath. Throughout our lives, we come to our own understanding of what it might be. For me, I envision an embrace through soft opal clouds, bathed in glorious rays of white light, where there's no more pain or suffering. Like being on the rise in an airplane when you break through the canopy of clouds, all of a sudden, you're somewhere completely new. A transcendent beauty. Love, wrapped up in an eternal love. I could be okay with Dad being in a place like that. He was taken care of, he was alright, and eventually, I would be, too.

Before family and friends started to arrive we had some time to let the dust settle. I felt most refreshed spending time with my sister's children. Their cuddles warmed us and we all pooled together to take care of them. They were dad's best buddies, my nephew having given him the nickname, Poppy, when he was young.

He had a stuffed turtle which doubled as a nightlight that he used every evening since he was a baby. It's shell would shine stars and a crescent moon on his ceiling. Naming the stars after the family became his nightly routine. "There's mommy, daddy, Nae Nae (his name for our mom)," and on down the line as he pointed to different stars, always ending with, "and Poppy's the moon!"

When my sister tried to explain to her children where Poppy went, his three-year-old mind simplified it. He figured heaven sounded a lot like being on the moon. After giving this some thought, he announced he wanted to be an astronaut when he grows up.

"I'm going to go visit Poppy!" he told us with a bright smile, his eyes electric. The kids often wave at the moon when they see it in the sky.

"Hi Poppy!" they say.

I now do the same. I think we all do. It helps us to see him there, because in a way, he'll always be around.

first healers

In our final weeks together, I asked dad any question that came to mind no matter how random. With the thought that I may never get the chance again, I didn't hold anything back. And neither did he. He answered each in his simple way.

"Where would you go if you could go anywhere, Dad?" I asked. He thought about it for a minute.

"I'd like to see the changing leaves on the Blue Ridge Parkway," he replied.

I had never seen it in the fall. He did while my sister was in college out east, but neither of us had driven the full length of the parkway just to look at the changing leaves. One guess where I decided to go first.

The road had already been my home for months, seeking healing over the loss of my marriage through the support of my community of family and friends. Losing my dad was another ordeal entirely. I still felt the road calling me, but no longer had the desire to see anyone. I wanted to run and hide somewhere secluded and alone. I wanted no one.

"I think I need to get away for a while," I told mom. "After dad's service I'm going to hit the road for a bit."

"I understand," she said as she hugged me. "Whatever you need to do. I support you. It's going to look different for each of us isn't it?"

Always the man with a plan, and an outline in bullet points just in case, dad roughly planned his own funeral since he knew the day was approaching. He chose the songs to be sung, the message he'd like to be preached, and asked friends ahead of time if they'd speak that day. Mom picked out the flowers for the service, my sister and her husband prepared a framed photograph that would sit at the front of the church in lieu of a casket (since his wishes were to be part of a body donation program for further research), and I put together a slideshow of family photos. We all found something black to wear and packed into the car to drive over.

I couldn't force the words out as everyone sang his favorite hymns, like *How Great Thou Art* and *Amazing Grace*. Neither could my sister, who was curled up under my arm leaning on me, reminding me of when we were younger. Nearly the same height as adults, she was always so much littler than me growing up.

Mom's Dad, our Grandpa, sat between mom and I holding his little girls hand. He barely spoke a word, in disbelief that his son-in-law went before him, being thirty years his senior. Yet, he was a steady presence for all of us, temporarily filling the masculine gap in our family.

When the wall of sound rose on the first chorus of *It Is Well*, I turned around to see the crowd of people behind us. It felt both surreal and crippling seeing everyone who loved him all in one place. I imagined his spirit floating through, surprised who his life had touched enough for them to be there. A colleague, patient, mailman, coworker, someone who volunteered for a cause alongside him, a friend—sometimes he was the only smile in their day.

"BUT IT'S NOT WELL WITH MY SOUL!" I wanted to scream. *Why did it have to be him?*

Dad's entire family flew in from Upstate New York for his service. The only surviving member of his core family growing up was now his older sister. Their mother, father, brother, and now my dad are gone. She shared an incredible bond with him, going through many trials as youngsters together. Even though she was just two years older, she stepped in as a motherly figure once their mom passed away, an event that would live with both of them throughout their lives. As brother and sister they had the same humor, mannerisms, voice inflections, and looked like they could be twins. Having her there felt like he was still with us, even if just for a moment. In life, they could share a look and understand each other; the only other person he did this with was Mom. The circle of people he let in was small, but his love for them was unwavering.

She and her husband brought their sons and they brought their children. Poppy's house, as we began referring to it, quickly filled to the rafters with familiar voices, stories, and energy almost like a holiday or family reunion. I had visited them earlier that year at their homes, and it was nice to receive them at ours. We ate meals together, played outside with my cousins and their kids, and shared tears over a man that meant the world to us. No matter how much time passes between visits, there's an indestructible tie that we're linked by and we pick back up like no time has passed at all. Having them there lightened the heaviness of that time.

Once they left town I got ready to set out again. Not knowing the full route I'd be taking yet, I packed all that I owned into my car. Sundresses, winter coat, and everything in-between. I stuffed it all into dad's red, white, and blue hockey bag that he gave me a few weeks before.

"You'll need a sturdy bag on the road," he told me in the garage as we looked at his sports gear and equipment spread across a tarp. Each item and every memory was painful. The years of pre-grief and the in-the-back-of-my-mind knowing he may be leaving us, and still, I never thought it could be possible. Even thinking of that loving exchange sent me into sobs. Maybe that's why I took it all with me.

I went about packing my cooler to its brim, which my cousin who had just visited gave me. The pantry at my parents house was full of items reaching their expiration dates, most of them having been purchased for dad. He had a feeding tube at the end of his life with special liquid food we had to order, so they were no longer of any use to him. Since none of us could stomach eating much when he no longer could, a lot went unused.

I'd scour the racks looking through dates on canned goods and made them last. I packed nonperishables like canned vegetables, beans, and packages of dried fruit. I didn't want to take anything that mom could use, so I tried to slim down the items she didn't want. Like the cream of rice she purchased in bulk because it was dad's favorite, a taste she never cared for. This became what I'd live off of during the time I was away. I formed an iron gut after the first couple of trips out, only getting ill a few times from expired goods. It was food, I was surviving, and I was thankful.

If I opened a canned item I knew that was my main course for the day. Whether it was black eyed peas, green beans, chili, baby corn, olives, prunes, or lima beans; I savored everything in the can, even the gross goo or juice that kept it preserved. I needed all the calories and nutrients it could give me since it was most likely one of the only things I'd eat that day. Being a vegetarian, the options were a bit more slim.

I also met folks around every corner who helped me. Truckers offered to buy me coffee and gas station employees gave me day old pastries that wouldn't sell. When I needed to splurge for a real meal I'd go for something heavy on greens and fresh vegetables, burnt out on the chip selection in travel plazas. Often the best place for this was picking up produce from farmers markets where locals would toss in a few extras for me. There were many forces that kept me going.

On my way to the parkway I stopped to see a friend I met a few months before. She invited me to come stay with her in rural Ohio and play with her horses. The night I arrived we bought junk food, talked about our families and boys, and watched mindless shows on TV. It was perfect.

The following day we went to the barn where she kept her horses. She taught me how to clean their stalls and refresh the bedding, which was unexpectedly therapeutic. I suppose since it's monotonous and repetitive.

"Cleaning up someone else's shit... who knew!?" she cackled. My entire body erupted with laughter, then I caught myself.

"That's the first time I've laughed since he passed away," I told her. She gave me a knowing glance and proceeded to tell me about her younger brother who died when they were young.

"He was my best friend. I don't think you ever fully recover after something like that," she said as she began to cry. "It hurts forever."

Caring for those horses became our quiet communion with nature and a remedy for my ailing heart. We brushed, bathed, walked, fed, gave them medicine, and even took selfies with them. Spending the day working alongside a friend in a totally new environment helped me forget about what happened for a little bit.

That night she gave me a present. A blanket with a landscape painting printed on it. It was a classic farm scene with a red barn, enormous green trees with a field to match, and a family of four horses in the front that I saw as symbolizing my dad, mom, sister, and I.

"Something to keep you warm on the road," she suggested. I've taken it with me everywhere since. It reminds me of her, that time we spent together, and how far I've come since then.

After departing, I drove to the northernmost portion of Skyline Drive in Shenandoah National Park in Virginia, which changes to the Blue Ridge Parkway further south. I left the passenger seat open for dad's spirit and imagined he was sitting there chatting with me, seeing everything I was seeing.

"Dad, we made it!" I yelled upon arriving at the beginning of the road.

Suddenly I noticed a large bird flying high above my car skimming the treeline. Dad was a bird photographer in his later years and would have been hollering for me to "pull over!" as he got out his mega zoom lens to get the perfect shot. I cried as I imagined soaring through the autumn forest with him. Red, orange, and yellow in my periphery, we flew through the sunset together.

I awoke the next morning, tears hitting my pillow, in my friends living room. I was staying at the home of my ex-husband's best friend from high school. Back when we were teenagers, they made the trip from their hometown in Virginia to Illinois often to see my best friend and I. Now many years later he has a family, a wife and three daughters, that I adore.

My ribs and back hurt once I sat up, realizing I had been crying not just in the dream that woke me up, my tears were real. It was my first dream about dad. We were in a crowd of people, and he was surrounded by new friends in the new place he was in and seemingly, had forgotten about me. I scribbled down detailed descriptions of everything I could remember; his face, his smile. He seemed so real.

Afterward, my friend started a fire in the fireplace and we talked as he got ready for work. When he left I could tell my sadness had rubbed off on him. He had known my dad well for a lot of years.

His oldest daughter sleepily stumbled out to join me, and was soon excitedly relaying all the news about their brand new pet guinea pigs. How they picked their names, how to tell them apart by their coloring, that she loved them equally, and how they never go outside except to go to the vet.

"They feel sick when it's hot out," she told me.

Her younger sister woke up and cuddled with their puppy and I under the pink fuzzy blanket I borrowed the night before, kissing the stuffed animal she let me sleep with. She put my gloves on her feet like socks for an extra layer of warmth and then the three of us checked our moods, and their dogs, with my mood ring. They reminded me so much of my sister and I as girls.

"Why are you up so early?" the little one asked me.

I told them I had a bad dream and how it kind of scared me awake.

"You know how one of your chickens died?" I asked them. One of their egg layers had died that week. They nodded. "That just happened to my dad. He died."

With a look of concern stretching across her young face the oldest didn't miss a beat as she cried, "Oh, your mommy must have been so sad!" I was amazed how wise she was at just eight years old.

"Yes, she is sad. We're all sad," I replied. The two of them pounced on top of me smothering me in hugs. They knew just what my broken heart needed—love.

My next destination was Austin, Texas, my home away from home. But, like memories of my dad were tethered to my hometown, Austin became the same with my ex. The neighborhoods we used to live in, the places we went together, being uncoupled in our friend circle of couples; it stings. Even so, I loved going back to visit.

The first night in town I made a trip out with a group of girlfriends. It became our tradition when I returned to meet up at a neighborhood bar to catch up on what life had taken us through during our time apart. We met at the same place every time, the walls covered in maps of the world, a happenstance homage to me, their nomadic friend. As a group we went through buying houses, new jobs, school, pregnancies, divorce, family illnesses, and loss of loved ones, both people and pets.

One of our biggest hurdles was yet to come: cancer. A friend in our small group of four was diagnosed. She's my age and the first of my close friends to receive that news. After a long hard road, thank heavens she beat it! There was a harmonious give and take of love and support for each of us in our darkest hour. No matter what, even when that storm rolled in, they were always there to welcome me back.

I made the trip because I was in a friends wedding. She was one of my bridesmaids, and now many years later, I would be one of hers. With heavy hearts my entire family made our way there, dad having died only weeks earlier. The bride and her two sisters, my sister, and I grew up together. They lived down the street from us practically our entire childhood and adolescence. We put on wild plays and shows for our parents when we were little, made forts in the woods (usually getting into poison ivy), and taught each other how to shave our legs when we got older. Their family is our family.

I got to town a week earlier than everyone else coming in to have some time with the bride before her big day. One afternoon we set out to go exploring at Hamilton Pool Preserve just west of Austin, a location we had always wanted to see. Arriving later in the day, there was hardly anyone else there. We talked as we hiked the trail to it. After months of not seeing each other there was a lot to catch up on. She was one of the first friends I told after I split from my ex. I had called her a few days after I left.

"Want to come over?" I had asked her.

"Yes! I've been wanting to check out your new place!" she said with enthusiasm. My ex and I had only been in our new apartment a couple of months.

"About that," I replied. "I have a *new* new place. I'll explain when I see you."

I picked her up and took her to my friends house where I was staying. The room I was staying in was nearly empty the day I moved in. The walls were a light lemon-lime green, one of my favorite colors at the time, and a queen-sized bed sat in the corner taking up the majority of the floorspace. I had a white desk, chair, and a quilt covered in bunnies that my mom made when I was a baby to add to the decor. I flipped it upside down so the white backing became my bedspread. As my first bedroom without a partner in ten years, I was starting over with a blank slate.

We sat in silence for a long while, both working on projects we had going; always doodling, painting, or something of the sort when we're together.

"So, I left him," I finally said.

I spent a lot of time with her and her fiancé after that day. Their small flat was one of those magical places where nothing changed when I was there with them. We talked about our dreams, made food and art together, and her fiancé was always playing guitar and singing. It drew me back time and time again; I felt more alive being with them.

Finally the trail opened up and we saw the pool. Half cave overhead with rock formations spiraling downward, part waterfall and a pool of water as still as glass underneath. We skipped to the shoreline and quickly took off our shoes, running into the water, our splashes causing noisy grackles to fly from their perch surrounding it. The sounds of our motions bounced around the walls of weather-beaten stone as rays of light hopped from one reflective surface to another.

"*Heaven!*" she declared with her arms outstretched like wings. Her joyful expression reminded me of how she looked when we first met, like she was four years old again for a second.

We sat on the shore to enjoy our picnic of carrots, hummus, and crisp green grapes, then laid back in the sand along the edge of the water to soak in the sun like cats with full bellies. When a shadowy breeze blew over us we decided to pack up and finish the end of the trail. The sunset that night was majestic. She was right. It was like staring into heaven.

Family and friends descended from far and wide and, as it usually does, the day of the wedding came faster than expected. After the ceremony, photos, and dinner, the roll out of reception traditions ensued. The cutting of the cake, tearful toasts to the bride and groom, the first dance, and then the one I hadn't prepared for, the father-daughter dance. Another bridesmaid that we grew up with reached out and grabbed my hand as the music began to play.

"I know," she whispered, her eyes filling with tears. We watched them glide across the floor and quietly cried together. Eventually, I would become the hand to hold for other friends watching their first father-daughter dance, those friends who also lost their dads. A club I never thought I'd be a part of, and one I'm not in alone.

I hung close to mom that night. It marked a big day for each of us; both single for the first time at a wedding. Even though the circumstances that brought us there were very different, never before had our paths mirrored one another's so closely. We decided to be each other's date; going stag, together. As the DJ announced the last dance of the night the bride's step-brother tenderly held his hand out to her.

"May I have this dance?" he asked.

A fragile look of surprise moved across her face. It's her fondest memory of the trip.

"It felt like your daddy was dancing with me one last time," she told my sister and I. "He held me close just like your dad used to. I felt his strong arms holding me up, holding me together."

I planned to leave town the day after the wedding, but wasn't quite ready to shove off by myself. I needed support and connection before setting out into the wild. I went to a music festival, shared meals, and visited my favorite art museums, all with friends I hadn't seen for months. Many of them had seen me through my years of turmoil. They threw my ex and I a going away party when we moved to St. Louis once my dad got sick, then a few short years later some girlfriends surprised me with a spontaneous divorce party the day I finalized it, and they were all there for me in this moment of loss as well.

One of my friends invited me to go horseback riding at the ranch she worked at that week. Having been a goal of mine since my time in the southwest that summer, I jumped at the chance; my second opportunity for therapy time with horses. She and I lived similar lives that year and became soul sisters through it. She left her husband a few months before I did, so each step of her process was slightly ahead of mine. I watched her living with friends, as she got a new job, and her own apartment; all steps I was afraid to make.

"If I can do it, you can do it," she told me.

Dust clouds rolled around us as we arrived at the ranch in her big truck. I could feel the grit from the air in my teeth and hair as I smiled from ear to ear. When I looked at my friend my chest almost burst with pride. She was a real live Texas cowgirl!

She introduced me to all the horses in the multiple barns, finally ending with my steed for the day. The trail she took me on went through streams, woodlands, and barren areas. It was a ride through the year we both had. We talked as we rode, overcoming pieces of our experience with every step our horses made. I felt victorious sitting on top of that powerful creature. Our backs straight, hearts open, and lungs breathing in the dry heat; we were warriors that fought our way through a bloody battle. I will never forget that feeling as long as I live.

Eventually I left bound for Big Bend National Park in West Texas, which I had visited once before. It was the first park I explored by myself after leaving my ex and it was again my first solo trek after dad's passing. Each sweeping landscape felt larger than my overwhelming feelings; its mountains and desert stretching higher and wider than my pain. It was the only place I had been that felt big enough to hold it all; my doubts, guilt, and shame, momentarily relieving me of the weight of them.

A friend once told me, "It's nice to juxtapose the lows with some highs," and that was exactly the feeling my soul found as I quietly camped out of my car in the Chisos Mountains.

The first day there I drove down Ross Maxwell Scenic Drive, a road winding through a gorgeous piece of earth, to a trailhead at the end. There was a long wooden pathway that led out to a stunning view of

Santa Elena Canyon where the Rio Grande flows between two gigantic limestone formations on either side. Due to a heavy rain the night before, the riverbed I'd have to cross to get to the trail had a higher water level than usual, causing deep mud pits where a path normally was. In my $20 boots, I braced for the worst and felt the mud and water instantly flood them on my first step. *No use going back now,* I figured.

After several failed attempts at finding the trail on the other side, practically swimming in the river with no other hikers to follow, I made my own way. Once I found the path I walked up a set of stairs carved in rock and then down the other side hopping over puddles as I went.

When I reached where the rocks and river met, I sat against a wall that formed a natural dead-end to the trail and took off my soaked-through socks and boots to let them air out a while. I lifted my shirt to rest my back on the cool hard surface of the rock and felt both small as a spider and tall as a tree all at once. This was a big moment for me; my first hike by myself and I was one of the first people out on the trail. A quiet morning hike would become my favorite way to start the day.

I stuffed my wet socks into my boots and carried them as I walked back down the trail, feeling the slimy mud squish under my feet and between my toes. I walked mindfully, being conscious of every sensation and smell, concentrating on the swish and flow of the river as it moved downstream, a familiar sound having grown up near the banks of the Mississippi.

Seeking seclusion, I found a spot to put my feet in the water. Hidden by a row of reeds, I made my escape. The hum of hikers voices passing brought me into a zen-like state when more people began to hit the trail as the sun continued to rise. I dropped my legs up to my knees in the cold water of the Rio Grande, laid back, and gazed upward to the space between canyon walls. At no point did they touch one another. The other side was actually a different country, Mexico. That's how far away dad was; untouchable, on the other side of the canyon in a whole new realm. I was glad we could still see each other. He was just on the other side of the water.

One of my favorite spots in the park became Dugout Wells, a small picnic area that's off the beaten path. There aren't spectacular views and the pass to get there is a bumpy one, making it a less frequented area. I rolled out my shawl like a tablecloth on top of a picnic table, laid on top of it, and picked at some lunch. My multi-purpose shawl regularly transformed into a picnic blanket, tablecloth, meditation cushion, yoga mat, scarf, skirt, a towel for a shower or the beach, and even became a superhero cape with my niece and nephew. It's so flowy and comfortable, pretty much a blanket with a slit at one end. Originally a gift from my sister that we got at the local flea market near my parents house in Illinois, it went everywhere with me.

Not a sound of another human for hours. The rustle of leaves overhead as I watched them flicker in the wind paired with the occasional clanking of a windmill made for a hypnotic pattern of sound. The occasional grunt of a javelina (a wild pig-like animal) coming from the surrounding brush no doubt scared the bejesus out of me, sending brief waves of terror surging through my limbs. I hoped they wouldn't have any reason, or ability, to climb the table.

My last morning there, I packed up my site and began the drive down the mountain and was struck with the brilliance of each summit, the sun barely peeking its face over the ridge.

"I would give *anything* to have one more moment with him! I wish he could see this. *He'll never see this!*" I cried.

Then again, maybe he could. I like to think that dad shared the experience with me. He had dreams of traveling in retirement but never got the chance. So, whenever I explored someplace new I silently began to invite him to see it with me. He had a window into my world and felt closer that way. We could see them together.

A town called Marfa, Texas would be my next stop. After the chill of an outdoor shower, I spent the evening nestled on a couch in a hotel lobby. From the flames in the fireplace, to the red orbs that hung from the ceiling dimly lighting the room, to the fur rug my bare feet rested on; everything was deliciously warm. A respite from the cold outdoors and my frigid car which I had been sleeping in. I became moulded to my surroundings in what was my living room for the evening.

The tent I slept in that night proved to be a harsh step back to my chilly reality, but the heaters in my bed sent a warm feeling up my legs even without socks on. I began to visually inspect the construction of my bedroom for the night. Silver metal bars fit together for the skeleton of the structure with sturdy cloth draped over the top, resembling a retro military tent (or at least what I think that would look like). As my breath inflated into heavy clouds above me, I imagined they were ghosts vacating my body; my thoughts frozen in midair. As I snuggled into my rented bed covered in brightly colored Mexican blankets, teeth chattering, I spoke my truth into empty space.

"I'm full, I'm clean, and I have shelter," I declared.

Warm tears turned icy as they rolled down my cheeks into my ears. Basic needs for survival. It's all I had left, like I had stepped back in time. In the middle of winter, in that tent in Texas, I could see how much my life had changed. Everything was different, whether by choice or taken from me.

Upon the recommendation of a friend, the following day my sights were set on White Sands National Park in Southern New Mexico. A mutual friend of ours had passed away that year, someone she was very close to. My friend said she pictured her sitting on a lounge chair looking into the sun on that never-ending white sand beach. It's how she pictured paradise for her. Somehow, she was able to leave a piece of her sadness in the desert, and I hoped to do the same.

After driving all day to see it, I arrived as the sun was setting. People looked like little ants along the ridges of sand dunes silhouetted against a multifaceted sky. The world felt so much bigger seeing how small each person looked in it. Footprints dotted the hills, remnants of the days travelers. The sand looked like large drifts of snow, and with the rapidly cooling temperatures, I questioned where I was for a moment.

I imagined dad sitting in a lounge chair next to our friend. They were talking and laughing together under the wide expanse of the desert sky. As every shade of pink, amethyst, and cobalt refracted from the sand like a giant prism, I thought, "Maybe this is what he meant by *"color."* I had never seen anything so beautiful.

I wouldn't be making it to my next destination before nightfall the next day, so I decided to take a slight detour on the way and stop at Chaco Culture National Historical Park in the northwestern corner of New Mexico. The gravel road to get there sent dust flying wildly behind my tiny spaceship of a car like the exhaust from a rocket, but slowed to a crawl when the gravel ended and turned to dirt. I got the feeling the rest of the way demanded four-wheel drive.

Another small sedan was close behind, braving the weathered road with me. We weaved our way gingerly through washed out portions, braced ourselves over cattle guards, and skated by ruts big enough to lose a tire in. Maude enjoyed the thrill, I on the other hand was praying we wouldn't get stuck out there in the middle of nowhere. After almost an hour on a stretch maybe fifteen miles long, we finally made it. The park greeted us with a road so new you could smell the fresh blacktop.

Old stone structures were built into the landscape here and there like some kind of cryptic ancient riddle. A section of stones that caught my attention had multiple circles within circles, reminding me of ripples in a pond. What had those circular structures been reaching for, what happened to all the people who lived there, and how did it become the ruins it was? All they left behind were some piles of stones. *Will that be all that's left of us one day?*

I ventured back down the same road as I exited the park, although it didn't seem quite as ghastly upon leaving. I had a better strategy of how to handle Maude over the holes and divots.

The thought of my car as a spaceship made me think of my nephew and his plan to go to the moon to see Poppy. Maybe that's why the drive back wasn't so bad. I was daydreaming about him and his grandpa playing in moondust; their bodies sparkling and shimmering as they ran together hand in hand.

what magic

Once my dad passed away I began thinking of all the things I want to do before I journey to the other side, a bucket list of sorts. The farthest my thoughts would allow me to go were locations. I didn't want to set my sights so high that I'd never reach them. I needed achievable goals, attainable places, even if they felt impossible at the time. With the resources available to me, they had to hold the possibility to flip from fantasy to reality. So, I made a running list of dream locations to see in the United States, the only stipulations being I had never been there before and could get to them by car. My wonders of America if you will:

1. Monument Valley, Arizona-Utah border
2. Arches National Park, Utah
3. Big Sur, California
4. Grand Teton National Park, Wyoming
5. Alaska, anywhere and everywhere

As I drove away from my home the day I left my ex, I envisioned driving through a dusty landscape with my saving grace, Monument Valley, on the horizon. Having grown up watching old westerns with mom while she worked on sewing projects, I always wondered, "Are those places real?" Handsome chiseled cowboys rode atop their stallions through the wide open scenery with those large rock formations looming in the background. Appearing to be painted Hollywood backdrops, those monuments became the lead characters to me.

I only knew the Wild West from photographs, paintings, and movies and had always wanted to explore those places for myself. When I looked over my road atlas of the USA as I prepared for the trip, I closed my eyes as I brought a pen down.

"Utah," I read aloud once I opened them to see where it landed.

I had never been there before and decided to renew my National Park Pass, an annual investment that paid for itself after stopping at a couple of major parks. It was this trip that I found out the National Park

Service was celebrating its Centennial year, which opened up my tunnel vision of my current circumstances and connected me back to generations before. What a perfect time to venture into my new life, on their 100th anniversary. To make the most of it, I would try to see as many parks as possible during the life of my pass.

National Parks would become my outdoor haven, playground—my cities on a hill. They offered solitude, challenging terrain, and my meditation and yoga practice blossomed. Experiencing them would completely change my life. As I began to look at parks out that way, The Mighty 5 (the five national parks in Utah), became my goal. I would conquer them all in one big adventure.

"*Freedom!*" I shouted as I flew down the highway after passing into Four Corners country; the only place where four states meet: Utah, Colorado, Arizona, and New Mexico.

"Utah: Life Elevated," the state sign read; my very first time seeing it. I created a new ritual upon this crossing: air high-fives with each state sign, usually making up a joyful jingle to accompany it.

The chambers of my mind expanded as they took in vivid color combinations and textures in the wide open landscape of the frontier that were all foreign and new. Maude zipped through bright orange rock corridors, past mesas standing like pillars that held up the sky, and around unimaginable crimson flatlands without a tree for miles.

When I looked at the patches of different colors of tar and cement that made up the road beneath me, I could visualize the symphony of people in its history and of every soul that had dared to venture west. Indigenous peoples who lived there and roamed the earth for centuries, the expeditions of Lewis and Clark, covered wagons full of settlers, the California Gold Rush, men and women who worked in the heat as they laid the network of highways and railroads, the tons of goods that had been transported on them, and everyone who's traveled it since. We were all connected, searching for our future.

The chill in the air took my breath away as it came through my cracked window, whipping my hair in every direction as I drove down long unending roads. My spirit was awakening. When I got close to where I'd be exploring the next day I stopped at a hotel for the night. Sinking my bare feet between those smooth cool sheets was marvelous! I spread my arms and legs out like a giant starfish taking up the entire bed, fully enjoying every second of being alone.

In the morning a heavy darkness covered the earth. White stars were sprinkled across the sky as if a painter had flicked a brush across it. With no one in town moving around yet, the woman at the front desk and I felt like the only two people in existence. After looking through the trinkets in the lobby while eating their continental breakfast, which included two cold cereal options, I hit the road.

As I drove, I turned off the noise off the radio, rolled all of the windows down, and listened to the wind. I was so close to the first of my top destinations; Monument Valley! It was a natural energy high like I had never felt before. As I came over a rise in the road, I immediately threw on my emergency flashers and pulled off to the shoulder. As soon as those rock giants came into view my automatic reaction was to slam on the brakes. I had to be still to look at them.

I could see for miles and miles in every direction! The road became a small grey line dividing the landscape that stretched on into eternity. It took an eventual turn to the right as it went around the massive monuments that burst from the endless ground. A thick roll of fog hung around each one; their blanket from the cold night. The sunrise cast bold hand puppet shadows from one to another. It was so far away that it still looked unreal, like a picture in a book. I waved my hand in front of my face to break the distance. I was really there. They were really real!

A few steps into the desert, I found the perfect spot to sit and watch the familiar scene from movies moving in real time. Once the clouds began to dissipate as the sun woke up, I began the day with gratitude; thanking all beings and systems that got me there. After several tears speckled the soil I walked back to my car and listened to the steady rhythm of my left blinker as I merged back into the stream of cars, all with the same destination.

When the road turned to go around the monuments I was absolutely speechless. The sheer size of them! They were so tall, and the road came so close that I couldn't see their tippy tops without sticking my head out the window. They were steady, unmovable, and sure. Something in the world felt permanent again.

I experienced my first tumbleweed as it moved across the road in front of my car on the way. I didn't know they actually existed! After one hit my driver's side door, rocking the car violently, I weaved in and out through the boulder-sized weeds.

"Dang! Those suckers could do some damage!" I told Maude.

Once I arrived I quickly got my coat out of the trunk. The wind blew briskly and seemed to go straight through me, causing me to brace against it. I ran into the gift shop to get warm and could have bought everything in the place; southwestern blankets and sweaters in all the colors of a sunset, knives inlaid with turquoise and mother of pearl, and painted vases made of clay. I found a pair of earrings labeled "dancing lady in the desert" that I had to have; orange, white, teal, and black stones in the most interesting and unique silver setting. They had a round circle at the top for her head with a long slender triangular body that swung back and forth on a hinge like hips. From that day on I wore them every single day, and they danced everywhere I went.

There was a rugged, rust colored dirt road that looped through the park that I was told might be unwise to take my low-lying vehicle through due to the previous days of rain, but I wasn't about to turn back after getting all the way there. I gave it a whirl and prayed Maude would make it. My music played softly in the background as I drove through the scenery like the classic films I used to watch with mom. Only this time, it was in full color.

There was a spot off the road filled with mini rock towers built by visitors who had come before me. The sun had warmed the valley, so I threw off my coat and replaced it with my shawl. I sat and made my own stack of stones as I enjoyed a can of green beans for lunch, my little tower of joy.

That evening I pulled into a town just outside of Arches National Park in southeastern Utah around dusk, thrilled to be knocking out the second of my wonders of America in my first trip. I drove through throngs of people visiting the area, shopping for gifts and dining out at restaurants. The combined smell of hot foods floating from chimneys filled my empty stomach. I chose the closest hotel to the park, which was undergoing roof construction. Luckily they lowered their rates accordingly. I would be out before they began work in the morning anyway. After scrolling through television channels and not finding anything, I turned it off and took a piping hot shower. When my head hit the pillow I was out like a light.

I woke up before the sun as usual, packed up my things, and was off. The park was open 24 hours so I figured I'd get a jump on the trails. The first sight was Balanced Rock and just beyond it, The Windows Section. There were monolithic columns that peppered the landscape circling them.

"What the!?" I shouted as I saw what looked like small animals sitting on top of one. They were people! Extreme climbers celebrating a morning victory. "How is that even possible!?" I wondered.

I hiked an area called Devils Garden, only slightly hesitant of it due to it's name. The arches seemed melancholic to me, my feelings reflected in the landscape. The top portions looked heavy, like for years they wanted to topple to the earth and get it over with. *"Can't you see we're in pain!?"* I heard their drooping forms cry.

Parched white trees twisted in agony, screaming toward the sky around them. Their bare branches looked like lightening striking from the ground upward in all directions. Startling me at first, small rabbits darted around sporadically. They were welcome company and became my pals I talked to.

Near the end of the trail I came to a sign that read, "Caution: Primitive Trail. Difficult Hiking." I figured I'd check it out and see how far I could get. Other hikers who were up to the task had gear to help with the climb. Once the grip of those same $20 boots started to fail me, I turned back. "I'm not meant to conquer everything out here today," I thought skidding back down the slick rock.

I most wanted to see Delicate Arch while at the park. The entrance to it was closed on the way in, but was open when I came back through.

"Hooray!" I yelled as my voice boomed through the car.

I jogged down the first portion of trail with no problem, then stopped dead in my tracks. There was a long slanted flat stone that people were climbing to the top of. The trail of fellow hikers seemed to go on forever.

"What am I thinking!?" I said to myself as I began the climb, not realizing I had said it out loud.

"We're just as nuts as you are!" a man replied as he motioned to his group with his walking stick, bringing smiles to all of our faces.

Once we got to the top the landscape transformed. Where there hadn't been a tree or puddle, there was now an oasis. It was like a mirage in the middle of the desert! There was a narrow winding trail along a cliff ahead. If the person passing in the opposite direction chose to hug the wall, which most did, I was between them and a drop-off with no railing. Being deathly afraid of heights, this was an extreme exercise in trust. Luckily, I recognized many of them having already passed each other on different trails that morning. They were familiar faces: comrades with a shared goal.

I made acquaintances at all of the parks this way and became part of a global hiking community. Often we'd give recommendations to one another, issue warnings about wildlife sightings ahead, or discuss trails we already met on. I never exchanged names with half of them, but we weathered and faced an obstacle together.

Finally a clearing opened, and there it was. Just as magnificent as I imagined, Delicate Arch! I sat in a round in what felt like a natural stone amphitheater with other onlookers watching as group by group had their picture taken underneath it; some with arms outstretched looking at the landscape beyond like they were ready to fly away, many striking various yoga poses, and families with small children that made me a bit nervous as they got near the ledge in front of it. *I'm good right here,* I figured.

I was so full of light as I sat there looking at it. It was a portal to another world. Like the eye of a needle, I peered through its opening, scanning the distant horizon to try and see where it ended. If only I could fly like those other onlookers pretended to be. It almost felt like I could, like mythical, inhuman things were possible there. A tidal wave of energy from years past pulled me under as I sat in complete stillness, feeling the vibrations of ancient ceremonies and offerings that took place there. A profound tranquility rippled through my entire body; a sensation of heat moving from my heart outward to my extremities and back again.

As the sun began to hang low, I decided to move along. I was heading to another park about 30 minutes away: Canyonlands National Park. My first attempt to see two in one day!

Could it be? The polar opposite of the last place I visited? Where the arches and columns rose to great heights above the ground, these forms fell beneath it reminiscent to the Grand Canyon in Arizona, many mini canyons. How was it possible for those two formations, so different from one another, to be that close together? It was like the land had an argument back and forth ages before. Small pools of water in the stone displaced the bright blue sky like polkadots as I walked through them; pools to a bottomless expanse. I looked out across the land to see what appeared to be dinosaur tracks scarring the earth spreading out like fingers. *Maybe they're the handprints of God. Was that where he gripped the world when he threw our planet into orbit?*

While traveling, I met an older woman at a supermarket one day. Although we began as strangers sharing recipes, she soon revealed more of her personal story. She told me about loved ones who had recently passed away as we stood in the baking aisle. Everyone was beginning to pass away—her family, her friends—everyone. She had reached another point with age that I have yet to. It was the time of life she was in.

"I don't have any tears left. I've cried them all," she told me. "My eyes have been worn dry throughout the course of my life."

I felt the same gazing into those deep gashes in the earth. I think my tears from the year I had could have filled each one to it's rim.

The next day I drove northwest to Capitol Reef National Park. I pictured it being some kind of prehistoric underwater reef due to its name, but was surprised upon entering to see old homesteads and fruit orchards. When I spotted a picnic area, I stopped to take in my unexpected surroundings. The sunlight sparkled across a small silvery brook flowing by the edge of a large grassy area I was lounging in. My mind felt lighter and brighter following new melodies of singing birds I had never heard before. The sun cast an intricate lace pattern over the surface of the ground as it filtered through the canopy of trees overhead. I felt delicately covered, as if by a warm afghan made by a family member, a priceless heirloom from Mother Nature.

Eventually I came to a fork in the road with a more weathered path off to my left. It had signs for a trailhead and warnings that the road would wash out if it rained. Being such a dry place, the ground would basically turn to concrete when it rained, causing a flash flood. The road I was considering would become a river. With not a cloud in the sky, I decided to take my chances. I had already learned some of the best gems were found off rougher roads.

At the start of the trail a narrow path dumped out into an enchanting arroyo. As I approached Cassidy Arch Trail, a sign notified me of rock cairns along the path to mark it, those same man-made stacks of stones I saw clustered at Monument Valley. In this case they were used so hikers wouldn't get lost. I began to follow them and was glad to stomp out some energy after a long drive.

I crossed paths with other groups at the start who were just finishing the trail, having been the early risers that day. After a while there were no more people and I began to wonder if I had taken a wrong turn somewhere, but the cairns reassured me that I was on the right track. Yet, steadily the trail began to look more treacherous. Butting up to the cliff was a one-foot wide bit of trail with a wall of rock to my right and a plummet to sea level on my left. Looking ahead, my route seemed to hit a dead-end with a large boulder three times as big as me directly in the path. Those silly stacks of stones no longer made any sense. I sat on a big rock and called it quits.

From where I sat, I could see a large portion of the gravel road I drove down to get there, then noticed Maude, the size of a mustard seed, in the parking lot. As I gazed at the towering rock formations that surrounded the canyon, one of which I was sitting at the edge of, they began to bend in toward the center. I was experiencing some vertigo, my fear of heights getting the best of me. After snacking on some celery with peanut butter and some chugs from my water bottle, my lightheadedness eased and I set off towards the beginning of the trail.

As I came back, a man bounded down a set of stairs, then crossed right in front of me to the beginning of the trail. Yes, someone had added their own set of cairns that I followed! The actual trail was around a corner. I decided to also hike the official trail, doubling my distance for the day. I laughed as I walked down the path with cairns clearly lining it passing families with young children. I should have known the path I was on was all wrong. Much too dangerous for most of the groups there that day.

I was grateful for the bonus trail and time to myself. My life felt the same. A lot of people questioned my choices. "You're going where? You're doing what!? It sounds careless and unsafe! It's not the easiest path!" But I lived reserved, normal, and had been responsible all my life. The role model and pioneer for my peer group when I was young, and juggling school, internships, jobs, bills, and holding down a household by and large by myself as an adult. I had worked behind many different desks for various companies, climbing achievement ladders I didn't know why I was on, and ended up feeling lost in the middle of it all. I was burnt out and more than ready to be outdoors deeply breathing in the freshest air imaginable on the side of that cliff. My soul had craved it for ages.

That night I drove southbound through Dixie National Forest. According to a staticky weather report on the radio, locals were bracing for a blizzard. I made a run for it, trying to make it through the pass before it was no longer possible. The snow began to fall around sunset. As the shining globe in the sky sank into the horizon, it cast its color on each iridescent snowflake. A rainbow of colors blew around my car as I pulled off the road and stopped to get out. Dancing in the flakes, now lavender and gold, I imagined being with my sister, catching a few on my eyelashes and tongue.

"It must be my birthday!" I could hear her sing out happily.

When we were little that was something our mom made up. The rest of the family had spring and summer birthdays. My sister's wasn't until winter, and half a year can seem like an eternity to a little kid.

"When is it my birthday?" she would ask. To help her understand, mom's answer was creative.

"When it snows it's your birthday!" she'd reply.

Dad took over in later years. "It's snowing! It must be your birthday!"he'd say, even if it wasn't her birthday. Any day it snowed was a day to celebrate her.

On her first birthday without dad, it snowed in our hometown for the first time that year. Big beautiful flakes rained down as if he were kissing her with each one. She ran outside with her baby girl on her hip, who had never seen snow before. The look on my sisters face was one of pure joy. A literal break in the clouds.

"Thank you, Dad," she said looking skyward as she began to cry.

I awoke the next morning around 5 AM in a semi-musty hotel room in Tropic, Utah.

"This doesn't feel like the tropics," my voice echoed as I said it to the empty wood-paneled room. There was an extra queen bed like when my family would travel to the beach. The night before my sister urged me to jump back and forth between them like we used to on vacation when we were little.

"Somebody's going to get hurt!" mom would holler.

"Oh, we're fine!" dad would shout back through a crazy grin.

Ten seconds later, one of us girls would inevitably start crying. The memory made me want to laugh and cry at the same time. Those times were so fun, but with dad gone it had become sad too. It sparked a pang of grief in my heart, its unfamiliar and unrelenting black leaves unfurling as they began to grow inside of me. It was Thanksgiving, and my first holiday alone, without my family. Looking back at the year gone by, I was having a hard time thinking of what to be thankful for.

We had a tradition in our house after everyone stuffed themselves around the Thanksgiving table. I think it's a common one across the country. Dad would wait for the last fork to be put down and ask, "What are you thankful for this year?"

We'd go around the table talking about everything from new friends, fun experiences and trips, to the occasional trial that we had grown from. Mom would clear the plates and bring out dessert, sometimes coffee or wine once we got older. We'd sit there for hours talking. I loved reflecting on the year behind us together. It's always been one of my favorite days of the year.

That morning I set off for Bryce Canyon and Zion National Parks in the southwestern corner of Utah, the final two national parks on my Mighty 5 tour. On the way, I drove by a school sign with a marquee that read, "There's always something to be thankful for." I made it my mantra for the day and began to think through the concept. The list in my head went something like this:

I'm thankful that I'm my father's daughter and that I got the chance to know him for thirty-two years.

I'm thankful for my marriage. It taught me about loving people, relationships, communication, and myself.

I'm thankful that my life has turned around this year. It's been excruciating at times, but somehow, I made it through.

I'm thankful that I'm on this trip right now and that I carved out time to take care of myself.

I'm thankful for all the lessons I've learned, new friends I've met, and old friends I've reconnected with.

I'm thankful for the breath in my lungs today.

There is always something to be thankful for!

When I entered Bryce Canyon National Park, a picture-perfect winter wonderland awaited me. Aside from the parking lot full of cars and the entrance station in the background, the welcome lodge looked like a secluded log cabin in the middle of the woods covered in a white down blanket of snow.

As I drove through the park I asked nature to guide me, reveal what I was meant to see. I came upon a sign for Inspiration Point (which I'd find many parks have) and stopped there upon an inner leading. I could feel the cold on the soles of my feet as I crunched through the fresh powdery snow up a steep trail. *This will be fun on the way down*, I thought. The pocks and turns in the undisturbed snow were smooth and gleaming across the ground, the sun blinded me between each split in the curtain of evergreens as I walked beneath them, and clumps of snow fell from their branches creating a hush over the earth.

When I approached the overlook I placed my bare hands on the icy silver rail around it, only hesitating slightly, wondering if they would freeze to it like when you put your tongue to cold metal. My hands didn't freeze, but the rest of me did as I looked out across the land. There were thousands of tall burnt orange rock spires protruding from the ground as far as the eye could see! Later, I would find that what I was looking at is fittingly named the Silent City. It's a tight cluster of slender rock columns that confound the mind. Each one has similar layering to the next like the three-dimensional patterning of a fingerprint.

Those columns are called hoodoos, also known as tent rocks, earth pyramids, or my favorite, fairy chimneys. Rising up in formation, they looked like the legs of synchronized swimmers all frozen under ice. My world stopped reeling for a moment and fell completely still as I looked at them. There was nothing else on earth except me and those chimneys, each one teaching me a different lesson all at once.

The power of creation voiced itself as they spoke to me, "Wonders are all around you! Come out of the dark corners within yourself. *Life is still worth living!*"

Even though a great silence hovered over my surroundings, I heard a message the spirit world was sending me like trumpets erupting through time and space. *I am valuable. I am just as gorgeous and perfect as any one of those formations, if not more.*

I had toyed with the edge of despair in recent days. "If I drove off the side of this road it wouldn't even matter. Life is pointless," I had decided. This moment began to erase that storyline. My tears fell like glass as I skated back down the trail to my car. Hardly picking up my feet once, I grasped onto the wooden fence lining the path, awestruck by my experience in that hallowed place.

Arriving at Zion National Park mid-afternoon there was a lineup of cars at the entrance. Although I thought it would be a quiet day in the park, everyone had the same idea that Thanksgiving. Families were picnicking everywhere with baskets full of turkey, fresh bread, and artisanal cheeses. Being one of the busiest and most frequented parks throughout the year, it was tenfold on a holiday. There were zero parking spots at most pull offs and trailheads; many cars already precariously parked.

The road snaked around the base of the mountain range in slow, wide turns. It was like floating a lazy river on an inner tube as the unchanging flow of traffic began to coax me to sleep. Beginning to get drowsy, I ventured onward to find a place to sleep for the night.

I stayed near a city called St. George after seeing it on the map, thinking of my dad since George was his name. I saw it repeatedly throughout my journey, and liked to think of these occurrences as guideposts, as if my map glowed saying, "stop here." I also met many George's and had to wonder, *Are there really so many in the world? Or was it somehow my dad stopping by to say hello?*

Deciding the granola I had wasn't going to cut it for my first Thanksgiving on my own, I went to a restaurant next to my hotel and ordered their $10 holiday meal deal to go. The woman behind the counter felt like a relative I was visiting for the holiday. As she fiddled with the register trying to assemble the perfect vegetarian meal, I envisioned we were sitting around a long table with a spread of food between us. She talked about her husband who was working the Black Friday nightshift and her five grown kids. I could hear in her voice how much she wished they could all be together that day, but they were planning to meet the following weekend for a belated celebratory feast. The same as my family since I was on the road and my niece and nephew had been sick.

I hadn't planned to go home at all. I was going to make my way out to California. I still wanted to make the trip I planned to take upon leaving Santa Fe, before my route, and life, made a complete 180. That is, until a phone conversation I had with my sister. She missed me. Her kids missed me. Her husband and our mom missed me.

After my divorce and father's passing it felt like I no longer had a family. Dad was the cornerstone of our family unit. He was the foundation, protector, leader, and provider. But he was gone. My husband was my family. He was my companion, teacher, lover, and best friend. But I could count on one hand how many times we talked that entire year. He was gone, too.

I was surprised when she asked me to come back for the holidays and special occasions at the end of the year. I didn't know I was wanted. I didn't know I was missed. She told me it felt like she not only lost dad when he died, she lost me. I decided to halt the trip right there and head back to Illinois for a late Thanksgiving. I needed to be with the family I still had.

When I began traveling I lost any adherence to a calendar or time and was no longer "the dependable one" as I had always been, often showing up late to important events. I wound up letting family and friends down when I had nothing left to give. Admittedly, I was sometimes selfish with my time. It was my first experience living on my own for just me, and at times I didn't feel ready to share it.

That night as I turned out the light for bed I felt a little lonely cuddling with a bed full of pillows. This night like so many others, I'd make a little nest for myself, inhaling deep into them hoping for the tiniest hint of a familiar scent. I burrowed deep into the make believe chest of a new man, running my hand across his chest. Didn't matter who, anyone would do to fill the hole I felt without another.

But then, I'd remember the countless nights where the ache of loneliness seemed to scream out of my chest when there *was* someone lying in bed next to me. I think that loneliness was bigger, more expansive, and all consuming. To fall into that kind of isolation within a relationship, within a marriage—to feel like no one is there when they are, that is the deepest loneliness.

There were two more scenic stops to make before my trip ended. Who was to say if I'd ever have the chance again? Life had gained a sense of immediacy in the weeks following dad's passing. I knew all too well that no one is promised tomorrow and seized each opportunity that came my way, never questioning my decisions or looking back. I was more than half his age when he died and had to consider, *What if my life is halfway through?* I made a promise to myself and to him that I wouldn't waste my life any longer. It felt like an obligation to really live since he no longer could.

I took advantage of a hot shower, my aunt on my mom's side once telling me it's the best way to wake up sore muscles, and made my way over to the lobby for breakfast. As I looked over the topping choices of the make-your-own oatmeal buffet, a woman complimented me on the coat I was wearing. It was an old school red and white puffy jacket representing dad's hometown of Pekin, Illinois with "PEKIN HOCKEY" embroidered across the back in big bold lettering.

"Thank you. It was my grandpa's and then it was my dad's," I said without a thought in my head. Having hardly spoken a word to anyone the entire time in Utah, I shocked myself as this personal story flew so freely out of my mouth.

She smiled brightly, as she replied, "What magic! You can take them with you!"

This exchange led me to open a dialogue with dad that day, trying to take him with me in a sense. Before he left, I asked if he would still talk to me when he went away.

"I don't know how that works," he said. "I don't know if I'll be able to talk."

"Do you think you'll be able to hear me?" I asked.

"I'm not sure," he answered.

"Well, on the off chance you can, I'm gonna be talking to you," I said.

"Oh, great!" he said sarcastically as he rolled his eyes, as if he'd never be able to get away from girl talk for a moment's peace.

He was a lone soldier in a house full of estrogen with mom, my sister, me, and all our little girlfriends growing up. Even our dog was female, and who knows about the assortment of fish we had. We laughed together at the thought. I sure hope he's heard me.

That afternoon I made it to Horseshoe Bend in Arizona just south of the border of Utah, a destination I hadn't planned on, but upon the recommendation of a friend, wanted to see. The small parking lot was packed. I weaved through the rows of cars a few times until spotting someone who was leaving. Unlike other places, I sat in my car for a while recovering from the high speeds of the freeway; my thoughts and innards still moving at 70 miles per hour. I sat until they were slowed down to stillness, then laced up my boots and hit the dirt lot more consciously than when I first arrived.

A short sloping path led down to the viewpoint. It felt like an outdoor mall on a busy day minus the shops. The pathway was congested, shoulder to shoulder, but I found the combined energy of the crowd to be exhilarating. The closer I got to that incredible u-curve in the Colorado River the lower my gut dropped. As I've mentioned, I'm scared of heights, always have been. I was afraid to stand too close to the large picture window upstairs in the house I grew up in. That never changed the entire time we lived there, and my parents moved when I was twenty-one.

Needless to say, I edged my way to the viewpoint very cautiously, wincing as I watched other tourists saunter right up to the end of the earth only to turn their back to the drop-off with selfie sticks. Mere inches away from their deaths! (Possible exaggeration here, but terrifying nonetheless.)

There was a trail along the perimeter that other people were walking that I wanted to check out for myself. I was curious to see the bottom and for some godforsaken reason wanted to get closer, so I crouched down and moved to the edge slowly, my body completely pancaked facedown on the ground. My line of sight fell across a cascade of charred rocks to the smiling blue-green river below. There was a boat taking tourists through the water at the base, their tiny faces looking up at me. I would have preferred their perspective. Every part of me was clinching and recoiling internally. I was acutely aware of my surroundings and highly focused on every sound, flurry of the wind, and gestures of others close to me.

"Done for the day!" I blurted out loudly as I mentally checked out of the situation I chose to put myself in.

I rolled over, dug my heels into the dirt, and began to carefully back away. There was an area with large boulders at a safe distance from the edge that I sat on for a while people watching, their collective movements making me overly anxious. Once feeling came back to my limbs, I chose to press on.

As I walked back up the path air began to reenter my lungs. It wasn't until then that I realized I was hyperventilating. My faculties were in a stressful overdrive and were going into protective mode. That whole fight, flight, or freeze thing is no joke. I completely froze looking down from those paralyzing heights.

My next location, Antelope Canyon, was only 20 minutes due east so I wouldn't have to drive far that night. After an exhausting day of stretching myself, I took an early night at a hotel and cocooned myself in the soft fluffy duvet on the bed, thankful to be safe on solid ground.

Mom told me about the canyons I'd be seeing the following day after watching a special about them.

"It looks fabulous!" she told me over the phone.

Our tour guide told us those canyons were found many years ago by a little boy who fell into one when he was playing. I tried to imagine how he must have felt as we descended into that place climbing down narrow stairwell after narrow stairwell. With massive rocks jutting out erratically everywhere, I wondered how he didn't break every bone in his body.

Beams of light found their way around curves in the crevices above us. Peeking through here and there they bounced off the walls throwing color in an assortment of warm shades whirling around me. The walls appeared to move as my eye followed the liquid rock forms, rushing, gushing, and swirling in circular patterns. Like the tides stopped during the crest of a wave on the ocean, turning it to stone. I turned to my right, looked up, and turned to my left; it was a gigantic mold of the water it was formed by. Once teaming with life, I was walking through an enormous fossil.

Fine hairline scratches ran parallel to the ground and each other, giving each surface the appearance of a huge pinstriped sheet blowing in a forceful breeze. Or like the organic forms created as a block of clay begins to take shape on a potter's wheel, with lines and grooves caused by their shaping tools. I felt disoriented like what I was seeing above me was below me, the aquamarine sky becoming a creek flowing between banks.

I could also envision that the stone walls were flames, captured in the highest definition by a slow motion camera. The vision so real, I began to move around points that flared towards me, so as not to get burned. When I looked straight up it was as if I was standing in the center of a great bonfire. As I spun around on one foot I kept my eyes toward the sky as the flames began to sway with my movements. White sparks spotted my vision from the swift motion and became embers floating delicately up to the sky. I imagine that's how prayers waft up to the heavens, like ashes drifting tenderly upon the currents of the wind, some cosmic force plucking them from the clouds like feathers, one by one.

As I began the drive again that day, my thoughts flipped through each mental picture. How was it possible for one place to resemble so many things; the sugary whips of frosting on a cake, a violent desert sandstorm frozen in time, and the texture of muscular tissue? I felt meager in the shadows of that place as the earth covered over me.

I stayed with a friend in Denver, Colorado that night. She welcomed me back to civilization with a giant hug, the first I received in weeks. We hadn't seen one another in a long time so it was a warm reunion in spite of the chill in the air. We played with her dog and bunny, she and her boyfriend took me out for dinner, and we all sat in their living room sharing tales of our adventures and all the places we hope to see one day. The travel bug got me on that trip. I knew as I talked with them that my life would never be the same again.

on the road with mom

Beginning to plan my long-awaited trip to California that spring, I asked mom if she'd like to join me for a bit and see some things she had always wanted to. The last time she made it to the west coast was on vacation with dad the year before. They explored Napa Valley and had a chance to lounge at the beach, go on a winery tour, and see the redwoods; a much needed breather during his battle with cancer.

"What else do we have going on!?" she said once she decided to come along.

My mismatched overflowing bags alongside her compact rolling suitcase were an outward expression of how different we are. As we loaded sleeping bags, blankets, and pillows into my car, it began to burst at the seams. Who cared about how it all stacked in the back? We were preparing for the time of our lives together.

We made a stop in New Mexico on the way to pick up a friend joining us for the ride out to the coast. The three of us listened to audiobooks together, stopped and got snacks every once in a while, and gabbed about everything new in our lives. We even came together to fix a problem with Maude. I bought motor oil and replenished it, my friend figured out how to reset the computer in the dash, and mom took her to a shop for the final fix once we reached our destination. What would have been a private trial, taking me much longer to do by myself, was made easier with their support.

As we crossed the border from Arizona to California, an ominous storm rolled in. From black to white, a complete tonal range of greys ran through the marbled clouds as the occasional ping of oversized raindrops assaulted the car. Thin, wiry cactus waved in the wind, bowing to the air like seaweed underwater. Moving shadows fell over plants that resembled large coral reefs, birds struggled against strong gusts as they swam across the sky, and the desert sands swirled over the road. It was like we were driving on the ocean floor.

We began our tour in southern California, making our way to San

Diego. Our first day there I sat by the hotel pool soaking in the sun. Palm trees bobbed their heads, swaying back and forth from side to side, dancing along with *California Love* by 2Pac featuring Dr. Dre and Roger Troutman being played by a DJ. I finally made it to California and the world was celebrating with me! Sunrays were like those emergency pads hospitals use to bring someone back to life. I laid my white lawn chair all the way back and let the warmth radiate through me. Laying there, my heart began to beat again.

Mom and I went out to dinner one evening upon the recommendation of a friend who traveled there for work.

"There's this great restaurant right on the water. I can't remember the name of it, but it has a patio upstairs with unbelievable views!" she told me.

We went back and forth searching for the name of the place until we finally found it; "George's", of course. As we sat down at a table overlooking whitecap waves crashing on the shore, mom and I made a toast to our George, both husband and dad. We spent the night celebrating his life and sharing stories of him, thinking about how lucky we were to be a part of it all.

On our last day there, after a shared breakfast and goodbyes with my friend, mom and I set off to continue our road trip. Our first destination was Joshua Tree National Park, a few hours east of Los Angeles. Long gone were my days of staying at hotels when I traveled alone, so I took mom along for a ride to see how I had been living. We arrived to a campsite with an opening, parked in it to claim it, paid the cash fee in a dropbox at the entrance to the camping area, and rearranged our items in the car so we could sleep in the back. I moved my things to the driver seat and floorboard and she moved hers to the passengers seat and floorboard. Hers and hers. Then we laid the backseats down flat and rolled out our sleeping bags side by side. All at once I saw the actual size of my car. The area we'd be sleeping in was smaller than a full-size mattress. It would be a little more snug, fitting two grown women into the back.

We went for an evening hike that night to investigate the new world we found ourselves in. Copper colored rocks towered high toward billowing periwinkle clouds, lifting our gaze to the mesmerizing twilight sky above.

"Dad would have *loved* this!" Mom said tearfully as she looked out over the vast desert, as if she could finally see the distance that was now between them.

"I bring him with me to all of these places," I told her, letting her in on my secret. "I imagine he can see what I see when I invite him to."

"I wonder what he's seeing where he is right now," she replied. Something perhaps only a partner could wonder.

As I held her in an embrace, I wondered how old I was when I passed her in height. With a smaller frame, shrinking more with each passing day, I could see the effect losing her soulmate had on her. It's like she was disappearing.

In the morning when we started to move around I could tell her body was a bit sore—she hadn't roughed it in quite some time. We noticed the age gap between us more clearly in the great outdoors. She was almost twice my age, and had been through twice as much.

We put the car back together and shoved off to check out the Joshua Trees. Neither of us had seen anything like them before. Large trunk-like branches sprouted from each other in an illogical way with tufts of spiky green leaves on each end; an odd dream-like spectacle resembling an illustration right out of a children's storybook. After our drive we found a nice flat stone slab to sit on for breakfast; cereal and some milk she got the day before. I usually never brought perishables along. My norm was granola or oatmeal with water. She brought some class to the desert.

We trucked on, north through Mojave National Preserve with the end goal of reaching Death Valley National Park before sundown. We had yet to have a heart-to-heart about regrets, unresolved hurts, and things we wish we would've said before Dad died, and unfortunately this was the day that anything stressing us came to a head. I don't know how the discussion became heated in the first place, I just know it did.

Her grief was different than mine. Of course it was; he was her husband, my dad. At the time she was moving through some anger about what happened, how it happened, and why. She was upset about issues involving his treatment, feeling as though somehow he slipped through the cracks of the healthcare system. She also felt confusion around some of her final moments with him. He said and did some things that were very out of character with all of us.

I knew it wasn't him. It was the disease, the embodiment of what was happening to him. He felt trapped in his own body. It became its own form of hell, a prison. It refused to function as it always had, and there was nothing he, or doctors, or any of us could do to reverse it.

At times he could be strangely mean. All of these changes brought out a strong resistance and even an anger in him we had never seen before. Caring for someone day in and day out only to receive this in return wounded mom deeply. After forty years together, there were moments where she no longer recognized him. He wasn't the same sweet man she fell in love with.

In truth, he was the most comfortable with her. She was his primary caregiver, facing the lion's share and most challenging portion of his care alone; the relentlessness of the everyday. For more than a decade she waited on him, cooked each of his meals from scratch due to his extensive food allergy list when he developed Crhones, ordered supplies he required, and drove him to and from doctors appointments and work in later years when his blood pressure dipped far too low for him to drive himself. Once the cancer discovery was made, she did everything in her power to make sure the household was together so we could all enjoy each other's company in whatever amount of time we had left. Yet, the one thing she craved most, to rescue him from what seemed to be his fate, was an impossibility. She couldn't fix it.

Only with her did he reveal his worst side; his torment, the depths of his very private depression, and a raw rage that his illness brought on when everything familiar began to slip away. She was his safe place, and when she served back her own stressors to him, he was hers. Always were. The part that hurt the most was that she never had the opportunity to talk with him about those things in an effort to mend them. At the end of a persons life, a lot goes unsaid. He was having a hard time breathing let alone have a healing or even rational conversation.

One of the last things he tried to say was an attempt to cover over those mistakes and things he wished wouldn't have happened between them. *"Forgive me,"* he whispered as he reached his hand out to hers. He didn't want to leave that way and could foresee the devastation it was going to cause. Regrettably, his illness had changed him, and he knew it.

I wasn't ready to hear her stories. It had only been a few months since he died, and although he was far from a perfect man, I went through a period of mourning where he was in my mind. I placed him on a pristine pedestal and wasn't ready for him to be knocked off yet. He was my daddy.

I don't know if it's because my mom and I are so different or alike, but we have a long history of having a hard time getting along. She is my biggest life lesson and at times challenge; the best and worst of everything. I believe if you ask her she may very well agree in reverse. The shift this time was that dad could no longer be the buffer between us. The classic, "wait til your father hears about this," threat used in my younger years now rang empty.

Dad had always been the peacemaker, a "peace at all costs" man even if it was a great cost. After an argument growing up, we would all go our separate ways, cool off, and merge back into life together as if nothing had ever happened. This led to having the same argument on loop, each of us falling into passive aggressive undertones causing distance between us. We never learned to face or resolve problems, they just bubbled and festered for years. When he died all of our roles changed overnight. The dynamic rhythm and stability of the four of us moved into an uncomfortable and teetering three.

Our energies clashed relentlessly like clanging cymbals as we continued the drive, and we couldn't get away from each other; we had another gazillion hours left in the car together that day. We went through some stretches of silence. Then eruptions. Silence. Eruption. Finally, at a rest stop we looked at each other.

"Can we start over?" I offered. "Neither of us wants to be miserable. Why are we choosing this?" And the day was different from there. We both needed to drop our opinions and try to see the world through each other's eyes. It was a delicate play of what was okay and not okay to talk about. With no cell phone reception, zero radio stations, and our ugly grief companions in tow, we did the best we could.

The land started to change the closer we got to Death Valley. My body began to cramp and constrict as we approached the park. My ex and I spent our last wedding anniversary together camping there. I had saved up for months, and after quitting my nine to five, we toured parks out west together for a month the summer before we separated. It had been a dream of mine forever and I finally made it happen, happy at the time to share it with him. It was bittersweet in hindsight. I was outgrowing him. It was a goodbye trip.

I didn't share this with Mom, leaving her clueless. That was the reason I was withdrawn. She had no way of knowing I was trying to prepare myself to return there, because I lacked the skills needed to communicate that with her. I didn't have space to talk about dad. I could only handle losing my husband that day.

As we arrived the warm air carried the distinct smell of rotten eggs as it wafted through our open windows.

"Sulfer!" mom exclaimed as her nose shriveled.

The colors etched in stone were lustrous; warm whites, cadmium yellows, burnt siennas, scarred occasionally with brilliant blues and purples. Unusual dark science fiction formations rose up and towered over us everywhere! We felt like explorers through an interstellar world of asteroids and black holes.

During the drive through we lost our appetites due to the combination of smells and heat. Camping areas were full where we were hoping to stay so we kept meandering, feeling slightly ill on the curves. When we drove by the entrance to where my ex and I camped for our anniversary the year before, I gazed down the dirt road longingly. A smile spread across my face and a burst of laughter escaped my lips.

"What!?" Mom asked.

"Oh, nothing," I replied. I was thinking about the last time I was there and silently replayed the memory in my mind.

We arrived on the night of our ninth wedding anniversary. Jackrabbits, birds, and bats bolted in front of our high beams as we drove down that dirt road to our backcountry campsite, like we were in a video game. There were no guardrails and we couldn't tell how steep the ledges were on the side of the road. It could have been the edge of a cliff as far as we knew! He was tensely manning the wheel with white-knuckles, our lights barely cutting through the thick black night. I was not envious of him in the least. It was an incredibly stressful piece of road to drive.

"I don't know if this is the most metal anniversary ever or some kind of omen," I recall him saying. If only I had a crystal ball to let me know it was both.

It's no wonder we were at each other's throats once we arrived. It was pitch black out, extremely windy, and our site was a pure sheet of rock. No tent pegs would hold for sure. With only the illumination from our phone flashlights we put that dumb tent up together cussing the entire time. Then we tossed our belongings into it to hold it still. I let out a long whimper of a sigh and looked up, about falling over as I did.

"Rachel, look!" he said.

The Milky Way was so crystal clear above our heads, it was like sparkling diamond jewelry in a case. I thought I could reach out and touch it! My forehead softened and body relaxed as I laid back on the top of the wooden picnic table next to our tent. How were we muddling around arguing with each other when all the while that was right above us?

That's the mystery of relationships. The first days and months when you meet someone are full of intrigue, elation, and passion. How could two people start there and somehow end up where we found ourselves? I pushed the thought away, as not to spoil the moment. It was just me and that sky. Everything else faded away.

I was awakened from the memory when I began to see signs for a steep grade coming up. "Brake Check Area Ahead," a sign read. I distinctly remembered the next portion of road from my previous visit. You drive down a long hill, descending rapidly, ears popping, until you come to a large open clearing with water to the left and an expansive dry plain to the right. It's different from anywhere else in the park. I disregarded the "No Parking" signs even though it's against my better nature to defy the rules. I had to get out of the car.

The wind swept off the water at the edge of the narrow road with commanding force. The car floundered like a small raft on a stormy sea as my hair and wrap entangled themselves around me uncontrollably. I raised my arms up and wide as if I was conducting nature's fury with my face to the sun breathing in deeply. I was reclaiming that place for my own.

Just up the road we stopped at a campsite across the street from the only gas station in miles. The wind was brutal that night, like a battering ram to our home on wheels as we tried to fall asleep in the back of the car. It felt like we were in a cradle being rocked (more like shaken) to sleep. There was a small outhouse to brave if we had to get up during the night. I held it as long as possible not wanting to face the elements, but alas, it was one of the coldest bathroom experiences of my life. With the gapping spaces between each wooden board that formed the walls, there was no getting around the breeze. But a girl's gotta do what a girl's gotta do.

Thinking ahead, mom checked the weather for our next destination, Sequoia National Park, nestled in the southern portion of the Sierra Nevada mountain range. I had been once before in mid-summer on that same trip with my ex. The smell of the forest carried us up the mountain and the all-powerful presence of those trees was intensely overwhelming. They didn't look real, like we were driving onto an immaculately constructed theatrical set. There had to be a trick of the mind. Surely we had walked into a fantasy. Those ancient trees couldn't possibly be that gigantic.

"It's six degrees there right now!" mom exclaimed.

We planned to sleep in the car as we had done thus far, but that was not appealing to her at those temperatures and it would only be getting colder as darkness fell. I saw the tension in her shoulders release as she reserved one of the only rooms left at the park lodge.

Sunlight flickered across the windshield and all through the car as we drove through dense forests and towns. Without makeup on my blonde eyelashes glistened creating a halo of light around everything in front of us. We passed lakes, inns, and restaurants that I envisioned people enjoying in warmer months, all closed for the season. As we approached the entrance of the park we pulled up to a guardhouse that divided the two-lane road. I had my park pass and driver's license out and ready, familiar with the drill.

"Greetings!" said the Ranger welcoming us. "Today we require chains for everyone entering the park."

"What!? We don't have any," I chuckled.

"You've got to be kidding," mom said under her breath, just loud enough for me to hear. There wasn't a single flake of snow on the ground.

"You can rent them in town a few miles back. Sorry, we can't let you enter without them," she replied.

Mom and I looked at each other puzzled as I made a u-turn around her hut. "I wish there would have been a warning about this," we agreed as we drove. The first few stores looked closed. Then we saw one with a large sign posted, "Chain Rentals Here," and pulled in.

"What do you want to do, mom?" I asked her.

"Let's see what it's all about I guess," she answered.

As she opened the door of the store an intriguing room of knickknacks was revealed. Bedazzled magnets, woven bags, and jars of local jam and honey were stacked on shelves with care. The distinct smell of fake pine like a large car freshener was a bit overpowering, giving me an instant headache. Luckily, we were directed outside for chains where a man helped us find the right size for Maude's front tires.

"Have fun and good luck!" he said as we left with our bag of chains. We were both giddy with laughter as we skipped to the car at the thrill of a new experience.

"It's an adventure, right!?" Mom laughed. One of those surprises in conversation that brought an immediate frog to my throat, eyes beginning to well up.

We went on many road trips as a family when I was a kid. Often we'd miss an exit, take the wrong road, or get lost altogether. Oh, the days before maps on your cellphone. After dad angrily threw out a few choice words, a bit of a hothead behind the wheel (to put it kindly), mom would softly reassure him that it was really no big deal.

"It's an adventure," she'd tell him.

Hence, his famous catchphrase was born. Whenever we started to go down an unknown winding country road, slightly losing our way, his eyes grew wide and a goofy grin would stretch across his face as he looked at mom in the passenger seat. She'd roll her eyes and smile back.

"Here we go again," she'd say as my sister and my expressions matched his in the rearview mirror.

"*IT'S AN ADVENTURE!!!*" he would holler, sometimes all of us in unison. The backseat became a rollercoaster car as my sister and I put our hands up in the air, laughing hysterically, our tummies tossing and turning over the rolls of the road.

We had a good laugh with the Ranger at the gate as we exchanged greetings for a second time.

"You're back!" she said. "A lot of folks turn around and give up on a day like today when I let them know about the requirement. You'll see signs letting you know when to put them on."

I drove the familiar road with a million switchbacks zigzagging back and forth up the side of the mountain like an old song I knew well. My ex had been driving when we visited there before. He was usually the driver. Maybe that's why I was so happy to take back the wheel of my life. I got a lot of satisfaction driving it the second time around and felt more connected to him with every turn of the steering wheel. Mom felt a bit queasy as my speed increased, causing me to slow, bringing me back from the clouds I was ascending to.

Along the roadway there were hundreds of waterfalls and small trickles off icicles falling from the rocks above.

"There must be a lot of snow up the mountain, huh?" Mom said as she leaned forward to look up through the windshield. Her face shone bright, her skin as delicate as fine porcelain in the cool blue light.

We watched the outside temperatures tick down rapidly on the car's dash as we continued to climb, eventually reaching a point where the water turned to ice as it covered the road. I pulled over at our first hint of slippage. The largest bracket of the chains barely fit. Chains the next size up would have been too big for my tires, and the set we had was almost too small. I had to take my gloves off to get a better feel for them and the metal was freezing! My hands were popsicles by the time I finally got them both on. We hopped in the car and reveled in our success for a minute, letting my hands thaw against the heat from the air vents before starting up the hill again.

The chains made a whirring sound as they gripped the snow and ice beneath us. I was a bit surprised that Mom didn't have experience with them. She was normally the winter expert, having grown up in Minnesota.

We began to see long wooden poles lining the path, spaced like street lamps reaching far above our vehicle. Initially questioning what they were for, we soon realized they marked where the road was for plowing. As we proceeded, the wall of snow was stacked so high on either side of us you could barely see the poles any longer.

Then they were all around us like a dream. Huge red trunks bigger around than the car we were in. The Giant Forest! It was unreal! The white snow provided a stunning backdrop, and unlike in summer with similar tones of brown and green surrounding them, they were separated from the foliage. They appeared even more massive in wintertime! Mom's first experience seeing redwoods was also during the summer. Both of us being in a much different time of our lives than our first visit, the shift in seasons was fitting.

Many of the parking lots that were littered with tourists on my first visit were now closed due to snow. The handicap accessible lot was the only one open to view General Sherman, the largest tree in the world by volume. The snow was so deep, the wooden fences that outlined the pathways to get there were totally covered, only the very tops of them seeable in some places. This allowed us to roam freely in ways that would have been impossible any other time of the year. Those trees stood around us like skyscrapers of a natural city. Visitors looked like tiny specks in comparison to their mass.

As Mom and I walked over huge mounds of ice under those giants, she felt like a friend I hadn't seen in years. We were both silent, the atmosphere summoning us to a state of reverence. That place had become an expansive winter cathedral as quiet as an outdoor library. Each tree pierced the pale sky like they could almost touch the robes of all the saints. When I stood perfectly still, I could've sworn I heard a choir of angels faintly singing. It was like we were given a direct line to another dimension.

That evening we drove through the camping area we planned to stay in originally. A place crowded with people in warmer months was a ghost town. Not one soul. The camping area my ex and I stayed in during my first visit wasn't accessible at all. The entire road leading to it was closed. Not plowed once, it was disorienting. That place, that memory, no longer existed.

After checking in at the lodge we strolled through the gift shop and spotted three sets of moon earrings and a bracelet. All made of hammered silver with a crescent moon pressed into them.

"Let's get one for each of us," Mom suggested. "One for each of us there the night Poppy became the moon." One for my sister, her husband, mom, and me.

That night I took advantage of the bathtub in our room and soaked for an hour in the steaming hot water, gradually regaining feeling in my fingers and toes. Before bed, mom tucked me in for the first time since I was little. She was now both my mother and my father. At fifty-nine, she became a single parent. We crashed hard that night, both sleeping better than we had in days in our matching queen beds.

The following day we went through the museum that was closed by the time we arrived the night before. We learned that the sequoia's reproduction and colossal size depends on fire. I thought back to my wedding dress burning in the woods, the only remains being cinders left in the middle of the forest. Then I thought of Dad's death; another trauma, another fire. Even though losing both of the men in my life seemed disastrous at the time, it made room for new growth possible. I was like those trees, like a phoenix rising from the ashes. I was stronger because of the fires in my life, and so was my mom.

We drove for many hours together stopping when we liked with Mom's house in the heartland at journey's end. The majority of it was spent talking about Dad. We time-traveled through every year of my life and before it as we pieced together the past; when my sister and I were toddlers, teenagers, my parents' dating years, when we were born, and the days just before he died.

"Remember baking cookies for daddy when you girls would get home from school?" she asked me. "You were both filled with excitement as he walked into the house. Just the turn of that key in the door sent you two into giggles. He would play along and say, "Wow, something smells incredible in here!" It was so fun surprising your dad like that." That one had long been buried until she uncovered it. I did remember.

Since we weren't on any schedule, we stopped at multiple beaches while driving down the coast of California on Highway 1, the Pacific Coast Highway, one of my all-time favorite drives. We had hoped to stop in Big Sur, one of my wonders of America, but the section of road to it was closed due to horrible mudslides. Our detour prompted us to slow down even more. At each shore we collected shells and wandered aimlessly by ourselves, each enjoying the alone time. We were a bit weepy at each place we stopped, both of us picturing dad enjoying the waves. The beach was his favorite place in the world. Most of the times we had been were with him.

"I'm glad we made this time together happen," I told her one day as we passed through Malibu. "I've been driving with dad for months, talking to his spirit, imagining he's sitting in the passenger seat next to me, calling out to any lone bird as if it were him, and now you're really sitting here with me. I love you, Mom."

She looked out her open car window at the endless ocean, the salty air whirling through her chocolate brown hair. It was like the clock turned back ten years when I glanced at her. The trip was feeding her soul.

"I love you too, dear," she replied.

A couple of days later we arrived at Saguaro National Park, one of the only parks near the limits of a major city; Tucson, Arizona. It's amazing how much the scenery shifts after just a few hours on the road—different state, different environment completely. We hit a small bend and were suddenly in a new land full of cacti five times taller than us! They were stoic, glaring intently at us from every angle.

"They look like aliens!" I stammered. She laughed and agreed, catching me off guard with a fabric and toothpick cactus costume idea.

"As long as you don't injure the grandkids or trick-or-treaters," I laughed.

"Maybe just a hat then," she chuckled.

We arrived right before sunset and quickly set out to find camping. Mom fell nicely into the rhythm of things. Having lived out of my car for a while I had a system to streamline prep and utilize daylight hours, but she added some tricks to the routine. It was her suggestion to add our yoga mats under our sleeping bags for an extra layer of comfort. Something I never thought of. She would have liked to buy a foam pad and make the hatchback as plush as possible. Since that hadn't happened yet, she decided to sleep on top of her sleeping bag, providing another inch of padding.

As I sat on a camping chair in the middle of the desert that night I could see her in the back of the car, it's interior lit only by her flashlight. She had her cheaters on, engrossed in a book that she was given from a friend. I was so proud of her. She was doing it. She was trying. She was looking for healing just like me and I was so happy to share with her the experience of what my life had become.

That night I had a dream that I went to the desert and found a hole in the ground. I fell into it and suddenly, I was traveling around the world seeing and experiencing everything I had always wanted to—all faraway lands across the ocean. When it was time to go back I came through the hole in the desert once more, only in reverse, my bag the sole witness of my great adventure. The life I left when I first went through that opening was gone. I had become someone different, someone new.

I awoke early the next day to hundreds of pale green glowing cacti illuminating Maude's interior. I got up quietly while Mom slept in and walked to a remote spot to sit on the ground for a while, drinking the cold watered-down hotel room coffee I made for myself the day before.

Still good. We had learned to make things stretch to enjoy them longer.

Reflecting on my dream as I ran my hands over the smooth desert sand, I was becoming someone new. As the sun burned brighter with my lightening mind, it woke me up gradually as it hid behind a big grey cloud. I grew to love mornings like that.

We drove down many dirt trails that day, stopping often to get a closer view of the bizarre world we were in. We inspected the lines of grooves and needles on cacti and marveled at the resilience of each new succulent flower. It was our second time seeing giants; first trees, now cacti.

Stopping at a picnic area for lunch, we found a table to enjoy the sounds of nature. We put together peanut butter and jelly sandwiches with a delightful prickly pear jelly she bought earlier in the day. Heat rose in clear yet visible waves off the asphalt of the parking lot. It was cleansing like a sauna, healing us from the outside in.

There had been many instances in my visits at parks where I saw older couples rekindling their longtime relationships in their golden years. As I watched them dance to love tunes played by pianists in hotel lobbies, hold hands down winding trails, and play footsie under the table in restaurants, I thought of how much my parents had hoped for that time and how much I had hoped for that in my own marriage as well. This trip was different, we witnessed and felt those sharp, heart-wrenching emotions together.

An approaching ice storm thwarted the last destinations we planned to make on our trip including Petrified Forest National Park in Arizona and Mesa Verde National Park in Colorado, but Mom was feeling tired and ready to get back to the comfort of her own home. The way I lived was my way of dealing with things, not necessarily everyone's. And although she enjoyed our time together, it was more of a refresher for her. A kickstart to help her merge back into the tasks of daily life. Later she would tell me it gave her greater peace of mind seeing how I lived on the road.

"After experiencing it I knew I didn't have to worry about you," she told me. "Not so much anyway."

Her initial plan had been to relocate to North Carolina after dad passed away. The two of them had talked about retiring there for years. They would spend their days at the beach, exploring the tree-filled forests nearby mountains offered, and we'd all come visit them often at their new retreat. She didn't want that dream to die with him. Eventually deciding against the move, she planned a family vacation there for herself, my sister's family, and I.

"This has been the best day ever!" my nephew shouted after his very first day at the beach.

"You are so right," I told him. "This has been the best day ever!"

Watching my niece and nephew's faces light up when they saw the ocean for the very first time in their young lives, all of us mourning and celebrating Poppy together, had been the best day ever. We all needed some time in the sand and sun.

I couldn't sleep one night and found a spot on a cushioned chair beside the pool at our hotel. No one there but me, I read the majority of a book a friend recommended, transporting to another time and place through the characters on the page. Reading other people's stories released me from my own life for a while, much like it did for my mom. Even though I was always traveling somewhere fantastic and new, reading was sometimes the only way for my mind to escape with me.

Once the pool closed at eleven, I went back to the suite mom and I were sharing. I sat for a while, grateful for the moment, for my cup of hot tea, for the room I was sitting in, for the trip, for my family, and for my dad who provided for us so we could be there in the first place. The moment shifted when I heard mom crying in her room. I knocked softly.

"Mom? Can I come in?" I asked.

A tearful, "Yeah," in response. I opened the door, light spilling into her dark room. "I'm sorry I didn't hear you come back," she said.

"It's okay. What's up, Mama?" I asked.

"I know I should be happy. We're having a great time. I just wish he could be here. I want more time with him. *I just want to be with him!*" she cried as she burrowed into my arms.

There were so many moments where I felt like a stand-in for my dad; his stunt double that entered the frame the night he died, literally filling his place in the bed next to her. My role this night was different. I was simply a friend supporting another who was in the deepest grief imaginable.

We went back to the beach the following day. My sister set up the kids' tent to put our gear in and it provided a shady spot to rest and reapply sunscreen. The whole family, including their dog, was there for our family day. My brother-in-law dug a hole in the sand for a make-shift charcoal pit and put together tinfoil packets of vegetables, chicken, and hotdogs. As we played in the waves our dinner slowly roasted.

It was nice to have a "man of the house" caring for us in that way. A big piece of our family was missing without dad, as was a smaller piece without my ex. Things felt incomplete without those missing pieces. My sister's husband did his best to fill the voids that day and we were all thankful. He's an exceptional being, daily tackling the wreckage that was left behind in the wake of our losses, and has become one of my closest friends. He's been there through it all, and was the only consistent male figure in my life for a long time. He's my brother.

When packing for the trip, mom walked by dad's picture at the house. It was the same portrait that sat at the front of the church during his memorial service.

"I'm taking you to the beach with me," she told him.

She wrapped his picture, frame and all, in bubblewrap and carried him in her red mesh beach bag everywhere we went; so he was with us, too. She only took it out once to sit by the ocean, holding him close as she looked out at the unfathomable surface of the Atlantic. It was one of the many heartbreaking choices I loved about her process. Her sorrow wasn't hidden in any way.

i hear you

On a trip back to Texas I decided to change my last name online with the help of a friend, finally making a private matter public. When I got married the change of name transition sent me through a bit of an identity crisis, but I grew to love it. Being in a partnership with another person was really special and sharing his name became an honor. Taking back my maiden name after that left me feeling conflicted. I had transformed and was no longer the girl I was when I had that name either. Why was the standard to have a man's name anyway? Unsure of what to do legally, I decided to go by my first and middle name. They had never changed since the day I was born.

One afternoon I got out on Lady Bird Lake and paddled through downtown Austin. It was quiet, my kayak one of the only things parting the water on a weekday. With each stroke of my oars through its satin surface, the lessons below bubbled up slowly. I began to move forward; one stroke, one breath, one movement at a time. The sun shone across the water as I made my own current. I was the only one steering the ship of my life.

A friend asked me to visit her classroom of third and fourth graders while I was in town. That week they were sharing stories about a time in their lives when something was hard for them and how they overcame it. We all sat criss-cross applesauce in a circle on the floor as my friend, their teacher, reminded them of the ground rules.

"We are to be respectful of everyone's time to share and good listeners of what they've been through. Got it?" she asked. We all nodded our heads in response.

They had hand signals that were explained to me, quiet gestures that let the person talking know we were connecting with them. Reaching our arms out front and wiggling our fingers meant, "I feel you, sending you love." An outstretched pinky and thumb, one pointing to them, the other to the person sharing, waved back and forth meant, "me too." Each child had a big story to tell, some things many adults have never experienced—things I have never experienced.

Then it was my turn. The day before my friend asked me to think of something that happened around their age to connect with them better. I shared that when I was younger I had a hard time with spelling. Learning my spelling words each week didn't come easily and was a struggle for a long time. Usually one of the first out in a spelling bee, it was humiliating. Some of them looked confused so I explained the word.

"I was so embarrassed!" I admitted. Many of them felt the same way as the hand gestures went wild. Then I told them how my dad helped me with it.

"How do you spell it, Dad!?" I'd ask him out of frustration.

"How do *you* spell it?" he'd reply. I don't know why I was ever shocked by this response. He gave it every time.

"Daaaad, just give me the answer!" I'd whine.

Instead, he'd make me sit and write each word out twenty or thirty times each. He wanted me to find my own answer. Even though I grumbled and growled in protest, somehow the repetition helped me remember and my grades started to climb. Maybe spelling wasn't so bad after all.

Then I shared another layer I hadn't planned on, but went with it anyway.

"Remembering those times is all the more special because my dad passed away not too long ago," I told them.

I was going strong until a few of the kids made the hand gesture "me too" with sad expressions on their little faces. They had experienced losing someone they loved in their young lives as well. A couple of us started to sniffle, myself included.

The boy who shared after me pulled his tiny child-sized ball cap down over his face as he tried to talk about his grandpa's passing. All the other children became absolutely silent, waiting to hear his every word. We both smiled through tears when he finally looked up. In that glance, no age separated us. We were the same.

In the months since he passed away, I encountered countless souls who had also lost someone that meant the world to them. My empathetic nature seemed to draw out the deepest stories from both friends and strangers, young and old. Since we had a shared experience, all filters were removed and we could be completely real. Whether they lost a parent, sibling, spouse, child, grandparent, friend, or another significant loved one, we understood one other and felt seen in the deepest part of our loss. Each serendipitous meeting felt like a happening specifically orchestrated to help us through it.

"Maybe these connections were always there but now you can see them in a new way," a friend observed.

In my experience, those of us in grief have the ability to see one another in a way others may not have access to. It could be a car mechanic, waitress, bus driver, coworker, the person in the check out line in front of you—there are stories of loss everywhere. If you haven't experienced it yet, one day you unfortunately, yet surely, will. It is universal as much as it is personal. When you're in the pit of it, you can't see that other people around may be struggling through something similar. It can be isolating, and profoundly, achingly lonely.

When I opened myself up to the universalness of it, the sameness of my heartache to my neighbor, friends, and even strangers that I met in daily life, that was when it started to break down and become more manageable. I'm the type that had to talk through it, and oftentimes healing came from interactions with folks when I least expected it. I've heard it said that grief is proof that love was there. It is the emotional, psychological, spiritual, and even physical embodiment of the memory of that love. Before I experienced it firsthand, I didn't understand. There was no way I truly could.

Many people I met along the way had tattoos to memorialize someone and each became a beacon lighting the way for me.

"I wanted a daily reminder of how wonderful she was," a cashier once told me about a heart on his bicep he got for his late mother.

A housekeeper at a hotel shared the story behind her "daddy's girl" tattoo with me after I saw part of it peeking from under the sleeve of her shirt, also having lost her dad to cancer. A woman at the front desk of a friends apartment building described the large winged back piece she planned to get in memory of her brother who died suddenly that year. It was their way of carrying their loved one with them.

Everyone kept telling me he would always be in my heart. To give myself a visual reminder of that, I wanted a poppy flower and a moon placed on the left side of my chest. There would be a triangle surrounding it, symbolizing our new familial trinity—mom, my sister, and me. I got it for his 62nd birthday, the first one without him in it. Thankfully it didn't hurt as bad as I was expecting.

"One hell of a first!" the artist said as she photographed and cleaned it. She told me in her experience, if someone wants a piece bad enough, they'll do it. As my first tattoo, and with her ornate and thoughtful design, it was most definitely the one for me.

It used to be tough to talk about my dad. Now I have a daily reminder that he'll always be with me. Whenever someone compliments the artistry I can tell them the story if I choose to. It could be sad, and it is. I miss him. But I knew an amazing human being and get to share who he was all the time. I wear it like a badge of honor and carry him with me wherever I go.

Once I stopped at a tollbooth out in West Virginia. I made a habit of pausing to talk when there were no other cars behind me and the attendant was up for it. I pulled up and put my car in park, window already down, and said a warm, "Howdy!" out my window as I dug for change.

"Well hey there! That's beautiful. What is that?" he asked as he pointed to my tattoo and motioned to his own heart.

"It's a poppy flower. We used to call my dad Poppy," I told him. As I spoke I looked up and did a quick read of his features. About Dad's age, even looked a little like him.

"Oh wow, that's what my grandkids call me!" he replied. "Texas huh? (Having seen my plates.) You sure are a long way from home young lady! You be careful out on the road, ya hear?"

"Ok, I will..." almost addressing him by his nickname, but couldn't form the word on my lips.

"Have a great trip and be safe!" he replied as he waved goodbye.

"Thanks Poppy!" I said as I returned back to normal speed.

When these instances happened, it felt like a brief visit from the other side. Everything is connected. Of all people, of course I pulled up in lane four and there was Poppy.

A new depth came to many of my relationships once I experienced grief myself, as well. One close friend revealed a new layer of herself as she told me about an accident that took her sister when she was young, a yoga instructor I didn't know told me about her own father's passing upon realizing my oversized clothing was my dad's, and a mother of two toddlers whose husband died unexpectedly, becoming a widow in her thirties; they became some of my closest and most cherished friends through it all. We weren't afraid to be vulnerable, sad, or cry. We could be raw. We could be real.

I also learned that grief comes in all varieties and shades. It doesn't matter whether the relationship with the deceased was a healthy one or not. I encountered stories where loved ones had been estranged for years. One friend told me his grief for his dad was different than mine. They didn't know each other like my dad and I.

"That's just the thing," he said. "Now I'll never get the chance."

While I was away, I comforted, and was comforted, by many friends who lost parents in Austin. I guess this is the time in our lives when that begins to happen more frequently, and we became the glue to help piece each other back together. When I got to town I planned visits with them, and it just so happened they would all be within a few days of each other.

One afternoon I swam at a lake with a friend and her puppy. We shared pineapple ciders, some laughs about past loves, and tears over the year we had, both losing our dads. I went back to the apartment complex I shared with my ex to visit another friend who's mom passed away only weeks before. We sat on her front porch like we always used to, talking, and this time crying, over our parents.

Another friend made dinner for me at her house. I watched the video slideshow that played at her dad's service that year; family portraits, graduations, weddings, vacations, and her family around the house. Although I didn't know him, he had a life like any other, and photographs were now the proof of his existence. I wasn't the only one with pictures to view with brokenhearted fondness, some poor two-dimensional rendition impossible to really convey the true look let alone spirit of a person.

I had experienced this at many funerals where I didn't know the individual who died, but only knew of them through their family and friends that loved them. You can't introduce someone to the person in a photograph. You can't hug a photograph. We sat stunned on her couch not able to believe that our fathers were now missing from our lives.

It's hard. I thought my parents would be around forever. I mean, I knew that everyone dies one day, I just pictured it being when they were old and grey, well into their happy and full retirement, and after they met my non-existent but potential children. When I would be older, wiser, and more prepared for something like that. In talking with my friends, I think that's what we all hoped for.

I hit the road westward late one night with my friends' stories filling my mind and car. I was planning on driving to Big Bend National Park, my hearts home, in West Texas for my third visit that year to camp for a few weeks. As I drove I recalled a friend who told me about a nature preserve of poppy fields. It was in a book she was reading, and upon looking it up, it was a real place somewhere in California! I stopped at a rest area and studied my trusty road atlas that resided next to the passenger seat. After some searching I located, "Antelope Valley California Poppy Reserve," just north of Los Angeles. I calculated the milage there and back with my phone. I could swing it financially, just barely. According to their website the poppies were in full bloom.

"What are the odds?... Why not!?" I decided as I let spontaneity take over.

Maude's headlights broke through the darkness down Highway 10 as I made the pilgrimage out west again. It felt like I had just turned around from there, because I had. On the trip with mom we wanted to see the poppies but made a change in our route once we found out we were too early for their season.

I had a desire, drive, calling, motivation, whatever you want to call it, to get there. My heart was wide open, adorned with my mere days-old poppy tattoo, and it was leading me to those flowers. I was unstoppable, pulling the rare all-nighter to get there. At this point it was muscle memory. I became a driving machine and "drove like it was my job," as one friend put it.

At each place I was attempting to connect with the earth, to find dad in a new way. I thought that if I saw that place it might give me some closure, even though I'd never reach a finish line when it came to my grief. Over the months I came to find that it will be something I deal with for the rest of my life. I'll spend forever missing Poppy.

Sometimes on long trips my thoughts would wander, contemplating what the road looked like from above with its cloverleafs, stack interchanges, spaghetti junctions, flyovers, and frontage roads. Such a bustling network of pavement and motion. Each person driving had a different story, destination, and group of people who cared about them. I was ready for liftoff with some Texas-style stacks, slingshotting far into the wild blue yonder to meet with plane contrails way high up in the sky.

Billboards advertised conveniences at upcoming exits, each a slight variation of the same chain restaurants, gas stations, and hotels; a continual Corporate America déjà vu. "Haven't I already driven by this?" I often wondered. Their consistency was comforting and lended to a sense of sameness, spanning an incredible distance across the continent. I had to get off the beaten path to find local mom-and-pop shops for that old-timey Americana charm. Roadside oddities like "The World's Only Corn Palace" in South Dakota, "Uranus Fudge Factory and General Store" in Missouri (yes, it's a real place), or "South of the Border" which sits just south of the border between the Carolinas were a true thrill.

Driving through one town or city sometimes threw me into a different place; an intersection in Birmingham, Alabama resembling part of Providence, Rhode Island. *"Wait a minute, where am I!?"* I'd think.

I would hang in the slow lane as I considered my dilemma, waiting behind a morning city or school bus, no time crunch to adhere to. Often I'd find myself down the lane of a neighborhood or a quaint subdivision in the suburbs of a place like Baltimore, Maryland assembling the perfect floor plans in my mind, considering if I would ever come back and buy a home there one day.

I received most of my news from the road. When I saw flags at half-staff I'd ask someone at the next stop what had happened or flip through the radio to hear what was going on. One of the bills I cut early was my cell phone provider. I only used it for maps and could make calls and send texts when I was on WiFi to save funds for gas. It was nice to be a little more disconnected from my phone.

During election seasons I usually had a pretty good guess of how things would swing, seeing signage and talking to people throughout each corner of the country. From north, south, east, to west, major metropolitan cities to small towns without a stoplight, there were clear patterns of party lines and allegiances. Bumper stickers and signs posted in front yards could sometimes be a way to keep my thumb on the pulse of things; giving insights to causes people cared about. Weather, traffic, local and international news topics, design, self-help, even celebrity gossip if I so desired; there was a station and podcast for everything.

Thankfully, I only experienced one close call during my time on the road, being nearly sideswiped by another car in Kentucky. That was the only one where I thought, *"This is it!"* for a second. When people say, "It happened so fast," they are not kidding. I had already learned everything was impermanent that year, we have but a brief existence. Having seen a number of car accidents circled by the terrifying glow of ambulance, firefighter, and police lights and a menagerie of blown tire incidents on the side of the highway, that one brought it closest to home.

I had run-ins with road-ragers and I'll admit, sometimes that may have been me, able to sense my agitation rising when I began referring to cars by the state on their plates. *"What the hell, Delaware!?"* But the biggest hazard I posed was when I was tired. If I grazed the rumble strip, tried to hold my eyes open with my fingers, or the most blatant telltale, began smacking myself in the face... I figured, "It's time to wake up and pay attention." At those times I learned to get off the road and either sleep, walk around a rest area for a while, or stop and get some coffee. By far my favorite option was to browse the glass figurines, camouflage clothing, and random B-movie titles in the aisles of a truck stop until I felt more awake. Sometimes while drinking that cup of coffee.

Often I'd see Maude's twin (the same color, make, and model) out on the highway and wonder if it could have been me from another time, perhaps from a few weeks before or maybe the future. Seeing her double going in different directions reminded me of how many options there are in life. It could've been me. I could've been going that way.

As the sun began to crest over the earth behind me, a glittery pink sheen reflected off my rearview and side mirrors and pinged off every reflective surface in the car. It lit up the road as the reflection bounced off the side of a shiny semi, so bright I had to pull out my sunglasses for the day. As it filtered across the road in a yellow haze, I imagined I was following dad's lead down the streets of gold.

After breaking away from all other cars around I went down a long winding hill and turned *Catalina* by the Allah-Las all the way up letting its beachy slow vibes heal me as I spread my arms out and wide, steering the wheel with my knees. I was gliding into the promised land, no more troubles or worries, they were all behind me in the rearview mirror and I wasn't looking back.

Giant white windmills were like the gears of my mind; hundreds of them turning and churning up all the old stuff, letting it fly away in the wind. Seeing them made me think about how they look under the cover of night, blinking their read beams in perfect time for miles and miles. Often I'd align the count of my breath with them. Inhale 1, 2, 3, 4, hold my breath for 4 counts, exhale slowly 4, 3, 2, 1, hold again for 4. I'd repeat this meditation often easing my thoughts and keeping me alert with something to focus on.

I passed by long rows of palm trees on my left, a grower's ranch for them maybe. On my right was a farm with a metal sprinkler system that ran the entire length of a field on big oversized wheels. There was a scrapyard with all kinds of machine parts welded together to make sculptures and fencing. Light wooden telephone poles passed by with the beat of the music, each carrying electrical wiring overhead, connecting one town to another.

The last few hours of the drive were a battle of wits. Although my entire body was giving out, I continued on out of sheer will. Maude rode sturdy and sure beneath me, finishing the drive. Whenever I felt scattered, she provided the only dependable straight line through time.

I had to reel in my overwhelm upon first sight of those endless fields of orange and purple, lest I literally fall apart. Droves of cars and people were along the roadside, so I continued on until there was an opening. Gradually, I came to a stop on the gravel shoulder, turned the car off, and put my head on the steering wheel.

"*I made it!*" I sighed, utterly relieved. After 20+ hours of road time I could finally sit still. I almost fell asleep sitting there but kept moving to stay awake.

Once several cars passed, I made my way across the road that brought me there, now on foot. A wide hillside full of brilliant orange poppies welcomed me. As if overtaken by their spell, I fell to my knees in a gentle clearing of them, laid my shawl out, took off my shoes, and succumbed to one of the deepest sleeps I've ever known. The only indication of how long I slept was the sun, which had moved to the other side of the sky when I reopened my eyes. I awoke to some people talking in my general vicinity taking a family photo.

"Right over here, *Dad!*" someone said as they motioned to where he should stand for a picture.

That one small simple word: *Dad.* It became a trigger that had the ability to completely, and oftentimes unexpectedly, break me. A child yelling, "*Daddy*, look at me!" at the playground or someone grocery shopping with their elderly parent, "What do you think of this one, *Dad?*" as they discussed the produce selection. Even my niece and nephew talking to my brother-in-law with a quick, "hey *Dad!*" at the breakfast table. It happened all the time. There was no getting away from it.

"Hmmm, Poppy," I thought to myself as I panned across the view before me.

I sat there for a while feeling the tiny flower petals and inspecting each of their fragile structures. I had never seen California poppies before. I didn't know there were different varieties. My steps became a prayer as I walked through thousands of them, my bare feet sinking into the bed of sand they grew in. I felt Dad's presence enveloping me, like all of creation wrapped around my energy field. For the first time, I didn't shed one tear. My system was too exhausted to produce them. It was a dry cry as I looked out across those fields, a deep inward spiritual cry.

I had every intention of turning around to head back across the country the same way I came, but thought, "I came this far, why not put my toes in the ocean?" I drove the extra hour and a half to the coast and parked myself at the beach for the remainder of the day. The temperature was cool, the water frigid, but laying in the sun long enough I began to warm. I was able to count the number of people out at the waterfront that day.

A friend invited me to stay at her house that night and I sat for at least an hour in Los Angeles traffic to get there. Not in any rush, I relished the company of people in the cars around me. I listened along to their playlist and radio selections as we sat, single drivers side by side. I wondered what they were thinking about, half tempted to ask out my window when theirs was rolled down.

Occasionally I did share moments with people in the vehicles around me. Once in a while I'd look to my left or right at a stoplight or to pass someone and briefly make eye contact with either the driver or a passenger. We'd find ourselves sharing a breath, maybe a smile, momentarily disabling our tunnel vision. *Oh, hello person. Hello other life, besides me.*

As motorbikes floored it between lanes a surge of air sent an abrasive tremor through my car. The world seemed to move by as fast as they were; continually spinning and changing at warp speed. As I sat I made the conscious decision to slow down and enjoy the ride.

While I was in town I reached out to another friend who had moved there recently. She was free the following day and picked me up for a day trip. Our first stop was for lunch at one of her favorite spots. She looked at me as we got in her car afterwards.

"Want to see where I grew up?" she asked.

"I'd love nothing more!" I replied.

We left the city and drove through the countryside for a while until coming to the exit for her hometown. As we came to a stop in front of her old house she said, "I can remember my mom tending that garden like it was yesterday."

She pointed to the one out front under a big picture window, tears beginning to fill her eyes. Her mom had passed away earlier that year. There we were, broken together. We cried a bit as she drove through a quiet natural area on a narrow curvy road. I looked out the window at the turns in the earth as we talked through hopes and fears of a future without our parents as guides.

Over the next few days I made my way back towards Texas and Maude hit a milestone on the way: 200,000 miles! I pulled over to document the speedometer and celebrated, dancing around her in the dark. I was on my way to another celebration, meeting up with a friend for her birthday weekend in Terlingua Ghost Town just outside of Big Bend. Earlier in my journey she helped me understand changing roles in a family as she spoke about the loss of her dad, which happened years before. She and her mom became more central in each others lives once he passed away. She helped me see my mom and all she was going through with greater compassion.

I arrived late on their last evening there. She and two of her friends were preparing a feast and I was so thankful for their rollout of hospitality. As we sat around a table on an outdoor porch, we picked up like we'd known each other forever. After their delicious home-cooked meal, I followed them along the edge of a dirt road that led to an old cemetery in the middle of town. With our flashlights scanning the path in front of us, we walked through looking at items placed on each grave for the person laid to rest there. Many were decorated with candles, flowers, colorful Mardi Gras beads, coins, six packs of beer, and toy cars. Some were marked with large wooden crosses on one end.

I had been there once before right after Dad's passing. As I sat on the ground baking in the mid-day heat that previous visit, those wooden crosses looked like a hundred church steeples pointing toward heaven. The sight reminded me of the lush green hillsides of the Bible Belt spanning across the band of southern states, with sanctuaries every few miles or closer, at times.

That night, I slept on a daybed in a quaint screened lanai off the house my friends were renting for their weekend getaway. I decided one day to have a room of my own just like it. Rooms that bridge between the interior and exterior of a house always seem to be my favorite part, that and the yard of course.

I awoke to mourning doves, crickets, and a menagerie of other creatures chirping and singing as the sun rose over the mountains of Big Bend National Park. The sky burned white, red, yellow, and blue, beckoning me to come. My adventure was birthed there since it was the first park I explored on my own, and each time I'd return made for another breakthrough. This time I was back to celebrate my thirty-third birthday.

Before we parted, the girls loaded me down with fresh food, extra water, and even a half-bottle of rosé to save for my birthday. We took a group picture on the steps of the general store in town, then exchanged hugs and goodbyes. I taped our photograph to the visor in my car along with a few other photos of friends to keep me company. Whenever I felt lonely, I'd flip down that visor to remember everyone that was with me in spirit.

I've explored many of the trails at Big Bend, the most memorable being Lost Mine. On a previous visit it was closed due to numerous bear sightings in the area. Open this time around, I got a later start on the day, even though the sky was beginning to shift and crackle as it held a developing storm.

Whenever I hiked unaccompanied I tried to drift behind another group of people if at all possible. Not right on their tail, but close enough for them to hear me holler for help. With no other people beginning their hike around me, I was regretting not purchasing that bear spray a couple months back. When a friend offered me mace for protection a few months later in Indiana, I took it no questions asked on the rare chance I'd have this kind of encounter again.

The sky began to low thunderously, but I chose to press on. Having been told how gorgeous the view was I had to see what was at the top of it. The path finally opened up to reveal one of the most breathtaking panoramic views I had ever seen! As I looked at it, a woman about my age surprised me as she hopped down from a high rock where she had been sitting. We took photos of each other with the view then walked back down the trail together.

We talked as we walked, our conversation finding it's footing on our past relationships. She had just been through a breakup and came out there to clear her head. Even though her separation was recent she had fresh insights for me. She was the embodiment of self-confidence and I stood a bit taller being near her. As we reached the end of the trail we decided it was a great day to move forward, having a deeper faith in ourselves. Meeting her changed the trajectory of my trip. I wouldn't be spending my time there in the mire of bitterness over my ex and all that happened between us. I was on a new path, one of forgiveness.

While at the park I saw my dad in the form of multiple strangers. I passed a bicyclist one day; same white racing shirt, black padded shorts, and helmet he used to wear. Growing up, I remember him being gone for hours on long rides. After a busy week at the office it was his release, his way to connect back with himself, nature, and to God. As the man and I passed one another in opposite directions, he gave me a salute with a wave. A gesture I remember dad making, one I had forgotten until seeing his ghostly double.

"You'll get a kick out of the downhill pass ahead, Poppy!" I said as we went by each other.

I met a birder one evening at the park lodge. He was there on a mission to see one specific bird, a Colima warbler. It's very rare, Big Bend being the only place it can be found in the United States, and is known to breed in the park that time of year. It's often located only through the help of an experienced guide. The day I met him he had just seen it! He showed me pictures as he feasted on a victory steak at the bar. His excitement reminded me of Dad as he flipped through photographs he had taken of eagles and other birds of prey.

I watched the sunset from Window View Trail another night. A man and his daughter joined me as the sun began to dip between the mountains. Listening to them banter back and forth made me yearn for more time with my dad. His daughter was in her early teens; they had so much ahead of them. As the sun sank, the sky ablaze in neon purple and pink between peaks, I made an inward plea that they would have many more wonderful years together.

One afternoon I stopped to read a bit at the Rio Grande Overlook and watched a storm move in. As it started to sprinkle I jumped in the car to drive the twenty or so miles back to my campsite. With the 45 miles per hour speed limit it would take a while. As I was driving, the storm I was watching merged with another dark front that was coming from where I was headed. They seemed to collide right over my head! The moment was so radical I pulled off to the side of the road.

I opened my door against a desert wind so fierce that I had to use all of my strength to push it. My dress flew this way and that but I didn't care. This was the reckoning. This was it! A gap opened in the clouds with one tiny ray of sunshine pointing down at me, like heaven had turned on a spotlight.

"DAD!?" I called out to him loudly. "Show me where to go!"

As the words escaped my mouth the wind nearly picked me up as it forcefully moved me twenty paces. When I arrived over a wilting, half dead cactus the wind suddenly broke. *"It looks like the whole world,"* I thought. I continued shouting back to the Sky, Dad, Spirit, God, Nature, the Universe, Energy... was *ANYONE* listening!?!

I screamed my inner rage, conjuring up every disappointment, fear, and dark place within me. Some of it just sounds; like a frenzied, caged, possessed beast was finally being freed. The violence of nature matched that of my inner monsters. I must have seemed out of my mind to any passerby, but supernatural powers were finally answering me. It was my first close encounter since my life was turned upside down. The thunder would boom loud enough to rattle through my chest and shake the ground beneath me.

"I HEAR YOU!!!" I yelled back at the top of my lungs.

Salty tears ran down my face and neck stinging my dry skin when I eventually sat down in a heap next to the car. I reached physical, emotional, and psychological exhaustion after being tossed around in the wilderness. While looking across the empty immenseness of the desert, I cried as raindrops speckled my skin and the world around me, feeling the same emptiness inside.

Once I got back to camp I laid in my car resting and contemplating all that just happened. Lying motionless, an awareness surfaced that each muscle and bone in my body hurt. My head, arms, legs, feet, everything; a deep ache consumed my entire being. I had agonized for months over losing my dad, my ex, and my old life; battering and bruising myself internally. The effects were making themselves overwhelmingly known.

I quietly listened to my new roadrunner friends; friends now that I knew what they were. I kept hearing their disturbingly loud call, at first sounding like velociraptors right outside my open car door. In actuality they were usually a great distance off, scurrying around foraging for a meal in the desolate landscape. On my trips to the park I also spent a great deal of time studying the movements of tarantulas and millipedes, always with a leery eye, that were busy minding their own business slowly crawling around between plants.

Suddenly an unexplainable flare lit up the interior of my car from the opposite direction of the sunset. I sat up to look out the back window of my car and saw the biggest, brightest, most vivid full double rainbow stretching endlessly in both directions. It seemed to span across the entire earth!

"Oh my goodness! Oh my God!!" I exclaimed several times as I fell out of the car.

I stood there in disbelief and thought of the biblical story of Noah that I had learned back as early as preschool. In my heart a new promise was made as I looked at the sky. I was hearing loud and clear that there was a force bigger than me out there that was going to take care of me. I saw it as a promise from Dad, too.

"Throw her a rainbow would ya?" I could hear him ask.

Sure, I'd talk to my dad while I was driving, pretending he was in the passenger seat next to me. And sometimes it felt like he talked with me. But this experience was different. All the anger I knew he felt about leaving this world, his family, and the life he loved showed up that night, and mine matched it. The resentment and feelings of betrayal I had about how my marriage ended made an appearance for good measure as well. Everything that happened erupted in that one spot in the Chihuahuan Desert.

Since then, it seems whenever I'm feeling low or lost on my journey, a rainbow is painted across the sky. The best part is, I never expect it. When I get to the point of desperation or start to feel nervous about my surroundings, there it is. I've been reminded over and over again that I'm not alone. There is someone or something out there that sees and is taking care of me.

Being one of the many firsts I'd face that year, I had been preparing myself in case it was a hard day; my first birthday without my dad. There was no one surrounding me with cake, candles, or celebration. I was by myself, planned for it to be that way, wanted it that way. Half of the reason I'm on this planet was gone and I needed to reconcile that in my heart.

I brought in the day at midnight on a cold morning my last night there. Lying on my yoga mat in the middle of my secluded backcountry campsite, wrapped in layers of wraps and blankets due to the chill in the air, I gazed at the night sky above me and watched as pure magic spread across it. Lyrid meteor shower, an annual occurrence, lit up the night with what looked like dozens of shooting stars. I stared at the clear dark sky full of twinkling dots waiting, then suddenly an unexpected line of light would streak across it. I followed each piece of wonder as they flashed intermittently and made a wish on every single spark.

Once I got cold and sleep began to seduce me, I snuggled into bed. Sifting through my days at the park, I tried to think of my favorite memory, a nightly ritual from my childhood coming to mind. Mom and dad would come into the room I shared with my sister, which was adorned in pink bows, and would stand between our matching twin beds.

"What was the best part of your day?" one of them would ask.

On this day, my birthday, and the first one without my dad, there were so many best parts from my time there that I couldn't choose one. I thanked a power greater than myself for showing me how loved I was through nature and by such a multitude of strangers. That trip turned out to be one of the best experiences of my life.

new "normal"

After spending a few weeks in my hometown of Alton, Illinois, my sights became fixed on the Pacific Northwest, which I had yet to explore on my solo expedition. This venture would be a departure; I didn't have a schedule or plan to stop and see friends. I was beginning to feel out of place in my own body, unbalanced, like a top wobbling before it tips over. I couldn't doggie paddle through the pain any longer, I was beginning to drown in it.

Every trip home seemed to have this affect on me. Most people thought it was high time to move on with things and get "back to normal," but there was no normal to return to. *Nobody wants to see this and I don't want them to.* I needed privacy in order to take a deep dive into my grief and hoped time would open up, even stop for a moment if possible.

Once again I packed all of my belongings, neatly organized, into Maude's trunk. Dad's hockey bag as my closet with clothes, books, cameras, and bedding, a cooler full of food in the passenger seat floorboard, and even the glovebox converted into my file cabinet with everything from my birth certificate to drawings I made of butterflies as a girl. After months of purging, all I owned was with me.

I buckled my seatbelt, double checked the essentials in the front seat like my driver's license, bank card, and keys, and waved goodbye to Mom who was standing in the driveway like she and Dad always used to together. We waved the "I love you" hand symbol to one another, my hand out my open window, until we could no longer see each other. It was tradition, one that pinged my heart in a different way this time around, not seeing dad beside her.

The feeling of leaving for a big trip is incomparable. What would normally be a drive through town turns into something wonderfully new. *What if I just hightail it out of here and keep going? Nothing is stopping me! I'm not turning around, not today.*

For this trip I would be retracing the path of the Oregon Trail from the Gateway to the West in St. Louis, Missouri to the Pacific Ocean on the west coast of Oregon. I decided to fall off the grid and turned off my phone, only turning it on occasionally to get in touch with the world. I'd be using my paper map to guide me. I wanted a respite, to withdraw from everyday life, and cut off as much technology and contact with the outside world as humanly possible.

There was an infinite bliss in solitude. Somehow, I had become a recluse that went everywhere, more of a recluse with people. I went through pockets of time where I felt alienated, the perpetual stranger exiled to a foreign land, and lost my ability to relate. Even though I was traveling hundreds of miles, conversation became difficult. My soul craved silence. No radio, books, or calls—only a giant void. For miles and miles and even days and days it wasn't uncommon if I hardly spoke one word. Maybe a "thank you" if I made a purchase.

My first stop was Rocky Mountain National Park in northern Colorado. Upon entering, I pulled to the shoulder to watch a herd of elk as they grazed. There must have been thirty of them across the road from me. I had never seen so many together like that. They eventually decided to move on, probably tired of being watched, and crossed in a single file line in front of my vehicle. They were so close I imagined I was one of them, walking slow and lumbering, following as they ventured deep into the forest to an undisclosed location.

As the drive continued to climb in elevation tall green grasses gradually became a bed of fresh snow; summer to winter in minutes. The plowed path on either side of the roadway created drifts the height of my car at times. The tips of dark pine trees poked up through the fresh snow and granite mountain peaks revealed only pieces of themselves, half covered in ice, as if a palette knife loaded with white paint had been scraped across the surface of a canvas.

Tall wooden poles stood like guards on patrol lining the road, similar to the ones at Sequoia National Park in California. The snow nowhere near reaching the tops of them, I imagined I was back on that other road at that other park, enthralled that it reached that high there. I pulled over to the shoulder when other cars came up behind me to let them pass by. I didn't care that I was going half the speed limit, if that, at times. I was taking it all in.

Once I finally got back on the expressway heading westbound, I chased the sun through the late afternoon into a real live perspective drawing. The blacktop was smooth like one long piece of ribbon candy striped in yellow and white lines to guide my way on. As the sun began to fall asleep, dusty blush and blue cotton ball clouds were pinned to the ceiling of the sky. Not one space between them. Fully covered in all directions.

I stopped at a gas station in Idaho to sleep that night, my first time sleeping in a parking lot. My funds needed to stretch as far as possible; the longer they lasted, the longer I could be on the road. The first thing to go was the price of somewhere to stay every night. This meant cutting out camping and staying at national parks whenever possible. I chose a 24-hour facility with a lot of people and movement going on, feeling safer with the bustle happening all around. As a light rain began to fall I hung my shawl across the driver and passenger visors to block out the blinding lights. As I stared at the water droplets on my side windows they became a thousand fireflies carrying Maude and I to a distant utopian dreamland.

When I awoke the next morning, I could barely stand my own smell, so I splurged for my first truck stop shower. Once "shower number five" was announced over the loudspeaker, I walked toward the back of the store with my duffle bag in tow, making my way down a hallway past a room full of casino machines and another stacked with washer/dryers, finally arriving to a bathroom covered in wall-to-wall tile which included a sink, toilet, and shower. As I stripped down and enjoyed the hot water over my body I pictured folks in the store browsing the shelves of state-themed shot glasses, snacks, and postcards. If they only knew what was happening on the other side of the wall!

At my first stop in Oregon I learned that the state requires fuel attendants. I think the only other place I experienced this was New Jersey. Having pumped my own gas for years, dad showing me how when I was a kid (which I realize is a big no-no now), it felt bizarre to need help. Once I accepted the change happening in this everyday transaction, it was nice to be taken care of in this unexpected way. Now used to the system, I drove over the black tube that rang a bell inside the station to notify the attendant I was there. A woman around my age came out to assist me.

"Hey there! I think I'm finally getting used to this whole attendant thing," I laughed as I opened my door. She looked at my Texas plates with a smile as big as mine.

"I traveled for a bit so I get it," she replied as she began to fill my tank.

While we waited she shared her adventures in backpacking for four years across the country, hitching rides on cargo trains. I had seen travelers with their large backpacks and bronzed skin walking to wherever they were going, which I'm sure was even tougher on the soul. I would have felt much more exposed and vulnerable if I were walking, hitchhiking, or catching trains across the U.S. I felt protected by my cars hard shell exterior, auto theft glass, locking doors, and four wheels to get away if need be. My small mobile home provided a bubble of protection that was a luxury in comparison. I likened it to one of those tiny homes people can't believe someone could actually live in.

"I have journals full of those experiences! It was both an awesome and trying time in my life," she told me with a bright light in her eyes. This dimmed as she looked down at her shoes. "The only reason I moved back here is because my boyfriend just died."

He was my age, thirty-three. The broader perspective that had become blurry in previous weeks came back into focus. We only live once, or for all we know, this lifetime only happens once. I told her the one sentence version of my story and that I felt directionless; I was just trying to figure out what my life was.

"It never fails, someone like you falls into my lap at the same moment I start to worry or question myself," I told her.

"Yeah, I was on the road for a long time trying to get my head on straight," she said. "Don't rush it. Take all the time you need."

She was the first person to say that to me. I had plenty of people telling me what the timeline should look like for my grief; how long was appropriate to mourn the death of a parent, a divorce, a move, and the loss of a job. Since it seemed like I should be moving more quickly over each hurdle, I always felt like something was wrong with me. *When was I going to get over it already?* She gave me the permission to continue on, exploring my own path. I was doing the work. I was trying to move on. My route was just taking a little longer and looked a little different, and that was okay.

The next day I went to Cannon Beach on the Oregon coast upon the recommendation of a new friend I met the night before. As I walked down to the waterfront I took in the smell of sand and salt in the air. It had been too long since I had last seen the ocean. A paper thin layer of water over the entire surface of the beach made it reflect like the surface of a mirror. Each person, cloud, and bird above it had a double below my feet; an alternate reality.

I stood in one place and let my feet gradually sink into the thick glassy quicksand imagining I could sink in up to my chest, letting it hug me securely around my rib cage. Not forceful, safe. When I glanced down I saw my own reflection looking back and flashed myself a smile. The woman I saw was beautiful and worthy of the life she was living.

A large dark land mass called Haystack Rock stood high above anything else around. When I got closer, small birds flew across the sky; never soaring, their tiny wings worked hard to keep them airborne. It was a large community of puffins! A bird that spends the majority of its life at sea, and a species I had never seen before. They moved with one another in surprising formations, exploding out of the rock they made their homes in. Larger birds with long black necks floated peacefully through them. I imagined them to be black swans.

That evening I pulled into a travel stop to hopefully stay the night. Noticing the signage that kept appearing at them saying, "One Hour Parking Only," I asked the cashier if I could sleep in their parking lot.

"Sure thing, we'll keep an eye on ya," he reassured me as he directed me to a far piece of the lot that would be best. Once parked, I set about getting ready for bed, steps I had grown accustomed to, my new life's routine.

After finishing a half can of baked beans for dinner, I got out, went to the trunk, and looked through my folded closet in dad's hockey bag to select pajamas for the night along with my outfit for the next day. I placed them in a small, more portable night bag, which previously had been his gym bag. Toiletries stayed in the night bag so I'd never forget them.

Then I went inside, changed in a bathroom stall, washed the day off my face in the sink, and brushed and flossed my teeth all with my shoes on. No cozy bathmat to sink my toes into. I couldn't be naked wrapped in a bathrobe in a gas station or out in the elements, depending on where I was staying. For the most part if it was hot outside, I was hot. Cold, I was cold. So I dressed accordingly for the night ahead. After finishing up in the bathroom, I went back to the car refreshed, with the soothing feeling of airflow across my clean face. At least that was clean.

There was something so freeing in allowing myself to be real all the time. A few years prior, I wasn't usually one to go out of the house without getting ready. Now I walked into a public restroom in full dress, makeup (depending on the day), and contacts and walked out in pajamas, makeup removed, and glasses; many times staying in my evening attire the following day. I became comfortable in my own skin as the world became my home.

Once I got back to the car my nightly preparation for bed ritual ensued. I threw my night bag in the passenger seat which became my nightstand; reserved for my purse, the book I was reading, shoes, and coat in case I needed to get up in the night. I laid my drivers seat down, released and lifted the steering wheel, and put on the e-brake to give myself more room. Then would shove a large pillow under my feet at the floorboard to lay horizontal. At different points in my journey, say if I were to stay in a camping area, I would lay the backseats down flat and spread out in the back.

Depending on how chilly it was, I might roll my sleeping bag out and zip myself in or just grab a few blankets if it was warmer. I always slept with the blanket a friend gave me, the one with the family of four horses on it that I received at the beginning of my trip, and often used a quilt made out of dad's clothes as a pillow.

I made one for my mom, sister, and I after he died. I hardly slept the week I worked on them. After collecting a pile of t-shirts, ties, flannels, and pj's from his closet to save them from being donated, I cried while cutting through each piece of fabric to make the square blocks. It became a holy pursuit with candles and sage burning around me. I'd dance and spin in the scraps on the floor letting the smoke wrap around me, cleansing the project and my heart. On days when my family needs a hug from him, we wrap ourselves up in those quilts.

The next morning I'd get ready in the same bathroom as the night before at a bank of multiple sinks, often with other women. It became girl time, like I was at a continual camp. I met other travelers, locals to the area, restaurant and gas station employees, police officers, carnival workers, homeless folks, and truck drivers; people from all walks of life. We got close quickly as I washed and shaved my armpits wearing only a bra or bikini top, depending on the season. I'd wash shirts and underwear with hand soap in the sink to get me by a little longer before stopping at a laundromat, then lay them out to air dry on the headrests and dash in the car.

I often played music on my phone while we got ready, leaning towards some of my all-time favorites like Willie Nelson, Fleetwood Mac, and Bob Dylan. New faces would join me at each stop and sing along. The lyrics from those old favorites became a unifier and often a conversation starter for us. No matter who's path merged with mine, topics flowed easily. When I looked at each of them in the mirror next to me, regardless of their story, I saw their humanity. I saw myself. When truly leaning into the moment, we witnessed a divine energy that connects all of us. In many cases, it was my only interaction for the day so I tried to show kindness to each person.

As I marched back into the store I'd take out a mason jar I had prepared full of granola and oatmeal, sometimes throwing in a handful of mixed nuts, banana slices, or a spoonful of peanut butter; "road oats," as a friend dubbed it. It was jam packed with protein and carried me most of the day. I'd fill my jar of goodness and a mug with a tea bag with free hot water from the coffee machine. On days I was unable to get hot water, I'd eat it cold and skip the tea. Then I'd top off my water bottle from the soda machine if there was a water lever or simply the tap. I would head out the door ready for whatever each day had in store without spending a cent.

A lot of people assumed I got some kind of inheritance from my Dad that I paid for my trip with, but that wasn't the case. He gave me a financial gift when he sold his business the summer before he passed away, but when he died I carelessly burned through it quickly (refer back to Utah). I had yet to understand living within a budget, the art of minimalism, or that I could travel without staying in hotels and eating out at restaurants.

I funded a portion of my adventure with various odd jobs while on the road, learning new skills like glass blowing, museum mount making, tent building, screen printing, fulfillment and shipping, working live music events, and house/baby/plant/pet sitting; landing me in a range of states temporarily from Kansas, to Oklahoma, Arizona, and others. The majority of my traveling money came from selling pretty much everything I owned. I hadn't taken much when I left my ex, not wanting the constant reminder that I was now without my life partner, but what I did take lived in the back of my car.

Throughout my journey I made trades for necessities like food and motor oil with items like my thermos, books, and jewelry. I also regularly stopped at pawn shops, clothing resale stores, and posted items for sale online in upcoming cities, then would meet up with buyers in pharmacy and store parking lots. The cash from those exchanges went straight into my gas tank. A little creativity and resourcefulness can go a long way. If it could help me get to one more place, parting with those items was worth it.

When I made it back through Illinois I sold my big ticket items that were in storage at Mom's house like my office equipment, excess camera gear, and even my wedding ring. It felt incredible throwing off the chains that attached me to things. I had no walls to hang things on, so why did I have picture frames? To accompany no walls, I also had no electrical outlets, so why did I own anything that plugged in? My priorities changed is all. At one time they defined me; representing my status, accomplishments, my ability to earn, and to acquire. But I was no longer willing to give them that power. My possessions transformed to dollars to keep me moving.

As I approached Crater Lake National Park in southern Oregon the next day, an icy rain began to sing as it fell on and around my car. The entrance appeared to be under construction when I turned in and a gate with candy cane red and white stripes ran perpendicular in front of me. Looking past it revealed the road had not been plowed. It was packed with snow. Closed. My first strike of defeat.

I grabbed my road atlas from its resting place beside the passenger seat. The wind seemed to blast through my door as I refigured my route. Cupping my hands and blowing air into them, I rubbed them vigorously back and forth over each other; the friction bringing warmth and energy back to my fingers. There was another entrance on the other side of the park! I'd retrace some of my steps to get there, but it was worth a try since I was so close.

Success! Stopping at the welcome center first since it would be closing soon, I learned the lake was created by a volcanic eruption and collapse, leaving a giant crater at the top of a large hill. The water is some of the purest in the world because there are no sources feeding it except rain and massive amounts of snow that it receives each year. The north entrance, where I first arrived, and a large portion of the drive around the rim of the crater were closed, buried in all those layers from winter. And I was there in June!

I prayed for visibility as I found a place to park at the edge of the crater and put on multiple layers of coats, hats, and gloves before running to the fence bordering it. I stood on top of a stone wall, the air so cold I thought my lungs might give out. The shadows of wispy clouds rolled over the bluest water imaginable. Not teal like tropical waters, but instead, the deepest merge of brilliant ultramarine and cerulean I had ever seen occur naturally.

Its surface was completely still, not one ripple or wave. So placid it looked like I could walk across it. I envisioned myself with the long flowing tail of a mermaid trying to swim all the way down to touch the bottom since it's the deepest lake in the United States. Translucent glistening ice encapsulated every branch, leaf, and pine needle in an array of frozen drips everywhere I looked. I walked into a living kaleidoscope as light bounced off every surface around me. A light breeze sounded like wind chimes as it moved through the crystal covered branches.

Over time, forceful winds had twisted and whipped the trees in haunting growth patterns around the perimeter of the crater. Drifts of snow resembled the sand dunes I saw at White Sands National Park in New Mexico, each place looking like the other. When inspected at close distance, each drift appeared to be its own mountain range. I imagined the Creator of all celestial spaces probably lived on Wizard Island, which rose up within the lake; the everlasting watchman who formed the pinnacles and phantom ships that parts of the park were named after.

As I drove the following day, I was escorted by lofty trees that ran along either side of a two-lane road. In the rain they became a shade of green so dark they nearly faded to black. Maude split open the opaque sky between them as she sliced through the air. Slowly the trees transformed into towering glass buildings in my mind, like I was in the heart of a city center, with people walking in and out of cafes and bodegas at street level. Then reality came back as I watched a lonely car disappear around the bend ahead.

The closer I got to Mount Rainier National Park in Washington, the more rugged the trees became. I was entering an enchanted forest! Lime green moss grew thick on every branch overhead, similar to how ice had encased everything at my last stop. The trunks of each tree looked like a centipede standing upright with hundreds of broken branches for legs reaching out, all wrapped in a furry green coating. Now new life surrounded me, growing as I was growing. Huge ferns blanketed the ground making me think of mom.

"I wish they'd grow like that at home! Think they'd notice if I dig up a few?" I could hear her say jokingly.

My visit there was shorter than expected due to cloud cover. Even at zero visibility, I could feel the mountain's larger-than-life presence as I watched teams of climbers inspecting their gear preparing for the tundra above. It overshadowed each of them as they went over safety rules and double checked the items in their packs. Only she knew what awaited them. *Maybe one day,* I thought.

While driving that evening, I tried to fend off hunger growls grumbling deep in my stomach, but finally decided to exit the interstate in search of something for dinner. As I ate I noticed an outdoor store dad used to like across the parking lot, the words "used to" ringing in a terrible pitch through my head. Since there were daylight hours to burn before stopping for the night, I went over for a visit.

When my hips pushed through a turnstile at the entrance, as if at a theme park, I looked up to see a large sign that read, "Get the perfect gift for Father's Day!" The heart pain I had come to know well gripped my chest. It totally slipped my mind that it was that coming weekend. It would be my first Father's Day without my father to celebrate it with, and there I was in one of the biggest dad stores of them all. Having already gone through the turnstiles there was no going back.

Every time I turned around there were cards printed with, "A gift just for you Dad," "Best Dad Ever," and "#1 Dad" not to mention everything in the men's section was essentially taken from his wardrobe. The exact pair of thermal socks he wore that I used to borrow, short sleeve dad-plaid shirts, the smell of the leather belts, and a stack of silly looking straw sun hats he would've loved. I looked around with tears flooding my eyes hardly able to see or breathe as I thought, "What would I get him this year if he was still here?" For a few minutes I tried to forget he was gone and pretended I was shopping for the perfect Father's Day present like everyone else in the store.

I found a long sleeve thermal shirt with the brand insignia that was his favorite. I bought a few like it, only with short sleeves, for his birthday a few years before upon his request. He had been sweating a lot from chemotherapy and thought something with a moisture-wicking element would work well under his clothing and scrubs at the office. That shirt is what I would've gotten him. I could picture the look on his face as he opened the box I wrapped with care. I almost bought it. Who knows why. Like it would do something in bringing him back? Or at least his memory? I don't know.

As I grabbed for the plastic hanger it hung on I was reminded of his boney shoulder as he lost weight rapidly in his final days. It was like it was his actual shoulder when I reached out and touched it. My other hand suddenly covered my mouth as I let out an involuntary, but very audible, gasp, and I quickly left the store.

Once I got to the parking lot I was an absolute mess, tears streaking down my face. I remembered a stack of old cards mom gave me, ones dad used to keep in a letter holder on his desk at home. She gave back cards that my sister and I gave to him originally. For whatever reason they were his favorites and once in a while I'd see him thumbing through them while he took a break from his work. I dumped everything out of my box of treasures. It's a memory box filled with old letters, pictures, and figurines that always came along for the ride. Flipping through the stack, I found a Father's Day card I had given him years before, probably when I first left home for college.

"I miss you and love you so much. Can't wait to be together again," my own thoughts to him read. Those words were never truer.

Having found that certain areas of the country were harder to find travel centers allowing overnight guests, I called ahead to a major truck stop outside of Seattle, Washington. I spoke with a woman that told me to simply ask for her by name once I arrived that night. She'd make sure I was taken care of. When I arrived I asked for her.

"Oh right, she works on the trucking side," a man told me at the general public gas station, as he pointed in that direction.

"Here goes," I said wide-eyed, summoning my courage, as I put Maude in gear.

The lot was huge and jam-packed with eighteen-wheelers resting for the night. It was my first evening staying in the trucking section of a travel plaza. My tiny white car wheeled slowly between their towering trailers, rows and rows of tires at eye level. I felt like a minnow in a sea of barracudas, breathing a sigh of relief when she gave me a parking spot in their employee section near the store and shower building, first letting me use their free air to fill my tires. I stood outside talking with her, other employees, and truckers for a while about their lives and the area. Eventually turning in as a light rain began to fall, using my earplugs that now lived in my door handle to block out the murmur of their conversation.

The next morning I left a note for the woman who helped me along with a gift from my box of keepsakes. I left small items like feathers, stones, and the like as thank you's across the country for people who helped me. Whether it was a place to stay for the night, a recommendation for something I needed, carwashes, showers, or food, I was thankful for every boost that kept me going along the way. Plus it was fun to leave something from Iowa for someone across the country in Washington.

As I drove that day I enjoyed one of my new favorite pastimes: scanning radio stations. I turned the volume all the way up for familiar favorites or sometimes let it play soft for a new song that moved me, often inducing tears. Music had a way of gripping right where it hurt, and since no one was watching, they took me for an emotional ride. I found tons of gems that I had never heard before this way and also landed on ancient relics that either made me burst into laughter while quickly changing it or relive a time gone by, often knowing every single word to the songs that made me cringe the most.

"Classic rock, who knows, country, top twenty, too fuzzy to make out, talk radio, fuzzy talk radio, an advertisement, Christian, local college station, top twenty twenty years ago, can't tell, fuzzy gospel, rap, oldies, classical, a sermon, another sermon, fuzzy country." I have a soft spot for old country music being from the Midwest, plus I'm a sucker for that steel guitar. Those stations usually provided the most fitting anthems for my drive across America. Each artists' way of storytelling through song coached me through my feelings. Even when I didn't know the words I'd hum and "oohh ahh" along trying to find the harmonies with Loretta Lynn, Waylon Jennings, Johnny Cash, Dolly Parton, and many others, making each solo a duet.

The occasional extreme weather alert series of beeps and white noise would interrupt my flow, but it added something unique to the ambiance. I enjoyed learning about each area through commercials, since they were always geared toward local interests. There was similar marketing in each city and state, but different sports teams, eateries, and attractions. Depending on what part of the country I was in stations varied slightly, the worst of it being when I was out of range. Twenty stations tapered down to ten, then four, then scan, scan, scan... nothing. In which case I would flip to a playlist that a friend made or listen to the wind awhile.

Once I met three girls, my angels in Nebraska, that traded their CD collection with mine.

"We've about wore these out!" they said. After listening to something fifty or more times on a road trip you reach a maximum limit.

The three of them were also on a road trip across the country going in the opposite direction and we happened to stop at the same place at the same time. Once we exchanged some small talk in the lunch line they bought my sandwich and gave me a bag of goodies from their stash in the car for my journey. I was so surprised by their kindness. They gave me compilations of R&B and top twenty hits, some of which were new to me, but my favorite was an album featuring a local a cappella group from where they were from. I must have listened to it hundreds of times, studying it, trying to find and sing through each different part of every song. We even took a selfie together, my first experience with a selfie stick.

When I arrived at North Cascades National Park in northern Washington, just south of the Canadian border, I found it to be rather quiet for midday apart from some large groups of bikers out for a weekend ride together. I wanted to hop on the back of one of their motorcycles and take in the place with no windows or doors; just me, the road, and wind flowing all around. Settling for the next best thing, I rolled all my windows down as the winding road carved its way through the mountains.

I was almost to the other end of the park when I saw a tranquil waterfall moving down a hillside. Barely glimpsing it out of the corner of my eye, I missed the turn and had to pull a u-ey. The small parking area had one lone cement barricade that I sat at the center of for an ideal view. Falling into a meditative trance, I listened and watched the water flow over large fallen tree trunks worn smooth from the continual progression of the falls, bleached white from many long days of sun. I began to see what those falls were trying to teach me the longer I sat there. The blow of events that year and my recollection of each would lessen with every passing day. They would become smooth and undergo a shift in color. Cluttered and broken, they would never fully disappear, but I would learn to flow over them.

After being on the road for a while my car was overflowing with receipts, trash, and other items I picked up on the way. Along with the clean up I decided to repeat a decluttering process I had done once before at my parents' house.

More than half of my belongings were reminders of my past and I wanted to let go of some of the lethargic energy I had been dragging around the country. The smaller my space, the smaller my need for things became. Since the back of the car was serving as my closet and bed the next few nights, some things had to go to have more room. A pretty dress from a special anniversary dinner out, the laundry hamper my ex and I used at our last apartment, and old pictures that would never bring me joy again, I collected into a trash bag.

I kept most of Dad's belongings, having become some of my most prized possessions. Just a miniature tape measure, but I remember him using it around the house when he worked on projects. Just an old plastic organizing box that held his bicycle trinkets, but he used it everyday when he rode. Those things were his, he touched them. Now that he's gone, somehow having them makes him feel closer. It's what's left.

My inner balance was off, torn right down the middle. On one hand I was trying my absolute darnedest to forget someone in complete and absolute entirety. He hurt too much to remember. On the other I was attempting to hold onto each and every of even the tiniest, most mundane memories. Every. Single. One. I tried to compartmentalize them, only wading into the tide pool of my double grief when I chose to, but it wasn't easy. I cried myself to sleep that night, one of many. It's a perk of being alone in the woods; no one to hear you cry except the trees and our friends in the animal kingdom.

The following morning, after eating a half-full mason jar of granola and water for breakfast, I brushed my teeth, splashed some icy water on my face, and decided against getting dressed. It was a pj's kind of day. I wasn't feeling well (got my period that morning—perfect timing as always) and the process of ridding myself of those things had drained me.

I walked over to an area lined with recycling bins and trash cans with my little white trash bag in tow. Once I thanked my items for everything they gave me, I threw my bag of old self into a large brown bear-proof dumpster, perhaps for other campers to dive for. I felt cleansed leaving those things behind, both my car and spirit lighter.

As I drove to Olympic National Park, situated in the most northwestern corner of the contiguous United States, birds flew in front of the car in pairs since it was spring. "Twitterpated" as my parents would say. Pale green trees folded back and forth, waffling in front of me like a life-sized popup book, as if nature was bowing to me and my pilgrimage. For hundreds of years they grew there. They watched as I passed by having already seen others go before me who were on the same type of self-defining trip. As their leaves rustled in the wind, I could feel the forest cheering me on. *Keep going! You're almost there!*

Upon arriving, I stopped to look at the most breathtaking view of deep emerald mountains that met shining golden waters. The soft sound of ripples as they touched the edge of the lakebed and the faint noises of cars going by on the 101 behind me serenaded my soul. I sensed that nature wanted to reveal a sliver of another realm to me.

Three daisies sprouted up through rocks to my left gently swaying back and forth in the cold breeze. They were my mom, sister, and I. Then I looked out to the mountains across the water and imagined it's where dad was. The three of us were rooted on the bit of earth beneath me, unable to move over the large expanse of water to him. I promised in that moment to travel and experience as much of this world as possible, before I also move to one of those mountains across the lake.

I continued to meander through the park, and upon seeing a sign for Ruby Beach, thought I'd hunt for buried treasure. Walking through huge towering fortresses of driftwood, I happened upon a peculiar sight. In a large rock with its base in the sand and surf sat a robin. Puffins had made similar homes, but she was out of her element. Miss Robin was making a nest in a small crack.

"What are you doing here?" I asked her.

She looked straight at me and made a loud call in response. She fluttered her wings and flew swiftly all the way to a tree stump at the edge of a thicket that lined the beach. Apart from her take off, I didn't see her wings flap once until right before she landed. She had the best of both worlds; a new beach house along with her cottage in the woods. She wasn't content staying in the forest. Her feathers appeared coarse and haggard like she'd been through a lot. My matted hair and make-a-home-where-I-am type of life didn't seem so strange after all.

As I awoke the next morning off Interstate 5 in Washington, the sky let down a gentle rain. It made tiny clicks and pops as it hit the windows and roof of the car. It was like having a house with a tin roof, a natural soothing noisemaker, one of my favorite sounds. Light peeked in through the windows around me refracted through the tiny drops. Without my glasses on it was like I was in a snow globe, seeing small hazy white dots in each one. The world was shapeless and soft, without structure or hard edges, giving me a firsthand experience of what some of dad's visions might have been like near the end of his life.

I put myself together, enough to go into the bathroom to finish getting ready. As I brushed my teeth a woman came to wash her hands next to me. She reminded me of my mom.

"Oh how lovely!" she said in a smooth voice as she wet her hands. "Nice warm water... almost scalding. Helps me wake up." She dabbed her face lightly with her wet hands as we exchanged some small talk, learning that we were both on a solo road trip.

"I've seen all of the lower forty-eight... a few times!" she said enthusiastically. Then she swallowed noticeably, the next thought was harder to say. "Well, you see, my husband passed away. We had always dreamed about traveling together. Going on a road trip across the country was actually his idea, and we never got to. I figured I could still do it, even if I'm alone." I paused for a moment to hold that thought, my mind slowing down to take it in.

"I got a divorce last year and then my dad passed away," I finally replied. "It got me thinking about how I was spending my life. I figured if I'm already halfway through it there's no time like the present to do whatever I want to."

"Yeah, I remarried after my husband died thinking my second marriage would be just as wonderful as the first," she said with a hint of disdain. "It wasn't. I got divorced, too. Sometimes it's the only thing you can do."

Her words held immense power for me. She was delivering a lesson in self-acceptance; to forgive myself for walking away from my marriage. Sometimes it is the only thing you can do. It was like I was talking to my future self and my mom all in one person—the experience of life after divorce combined with the loss of a spouse in death. I wasn't the only one looking for healing on the road, and I knew after talking with her that there were most likely a lot more people out there just like us.

My next destination was back down to Seattle to see a friend. I was coming through on Father's Day weekend and apologized to her ahead of time if I was a wreck. After my episode at the outdoor store, I knew I was in for a doozy. She cued up one of her favorite shows called *This Is Us* to binge watch and made heaping bowls of pasta for dinner with chocolate ice cream for dessert. I was thankful to be with her in one of my lowest moments. We sat together and bawled through the ups and downs of the emotional show which is sewn together by a story of father loss. It was so healing to do together.

Originally, I planned to go to the early service at her church on Father's Day, but since my friend was working in the nursery, I sat through the sermon twice. It hit me like a lightening bolt. The message was about how God can be a Father to the fatherless and about finding hope when faced with troubles and sorrow in life. I sat as still as a stone; it was like it was written for me. It was exactly what I needed on that really hard day, a large dose of hope.

When we got back to my friend's house she called her dad for the holiday. She told me before she did so, offering me the out if it would be too much to overhear. I didn't think it would bother me. What caught me off guard was that both of her parents got on the line. She talked back and forth directing the conversation to mom, then to dad. I had forgotten we used to do that.

She expressed fears about her own father's health once she was off the phone. That couch of hers saw a lot of tears from the two of us that weekend. It was a kind of therapy.

About a year later I got the news. After battling illness for years, her dad also passed away. Every future Father's Day would now be different for her as well. I wished with everything in me that I could take away that reality for her. A stinging hits me with each friend who experiences it.

There goes another, and another; when someone that was central to their existence disappears. That excruciating moment when everything changes.

While I was in town she and some girlfriends organized a hike for us at Melmont Ghost Town, a wild overgrown trail with long since abandoned stone buildings a little over an hour south of the city. On the drive to get there, we talked about everything under the sun, eventually landing on my trip and where I wanted to go next.

"Well, I was hoping to go to Alaska, but I can't figure out the route," I told them. I surmised that it was probably impossible to drive there; fearful about going through another country, driving that incredible distance all by myself, getting lost, and I knew nothing about the weather conditions that time of year. I felt too unprepared to cross into Canada without more extensive research, and I'm not really a research type of gal. The list of "what if's" seemed too long to follow through.

"Do you have your passport with you?" one of them asked me.

"I do! I brought it with me just in case," I replied.

"Well, we've both lived there! We can help you with what roads to take and this is the perfect time of year!" they said. I couldn't believe it. The two women sitting in the backseat gave me directions, told me where in Anchorage to stop for the best pizza, and about not to be missed sights while driving through.

Months before I looked at my road atlas with the list of my top five destinations in the USA, Alaska being the most intimidating and seemingly unattainable.

"Denali National Park," I read out loud as I marked it with a big star. It's one of eight national park's in Alaska and sits in the center of the state. It would be the culmination of my trip if I could make it there and became the desire of my heart. Going to Alaska had been a dream of mine since I was in grade school. I remember learning about the fifty states in class and seeing how far away the "North to the Future" state was.

"I'll never get all the way up there. It's too far," I said to myself.

If ever I felt a Divine calling on my journey, this was it. As I recalled my doubts as a girl I decided, I was going to Alaska!

a world away

Once I passed the exit I took on my trip to North Cascades National Park, every road and sight before me would be new. Air sailed under, over, around, and through my freedom mobile. Everything inside of me shook with excitement, yet my hands remained calm. Steady on, ever forward.

I arrived to the Canadian border more quickly than expected, got my passport out and ready, was asked a few specifics about the reason for my trip, then directed inside for further questioning. Border patrol was having a hard time understanding the simplicity behind my wish to check Alaska off my "states visited" list.

"No really, that's the only reason I'm crossing through Canada," I told the officer at the counter. He looked at me over my passport with a chuckle.

"Alright girl, do your thing," he said as he handed it back to me.

When I passed under a cement overhang that resembled a large bank teller drive-thru, I realized it was the first time I was in a different country all by myself! Electricity flowed through my veins, I was so excited! I kissed my fingertips and touched Maude's ceiling with them.

"We're doing it!" I told her. Just then the theme from *Rocky*, *Gonna Fly Now* by Bill Conti, came over the speakers on a staticky radio station.

Laughter bubbled up from the very core of me, a deep hearty belly laugh. It was the happiest I had been all year. I pictured myself running swiftly down that road, away from my past, away from that year; the distance separating me monumental. I could feel my strength building as I began to soar. I was flying away from it all.

As I drove north up the Trans-Canada Highway through British Columbia, towns with ironic names were in my path. In order, I went through Bridal Falls, Hope, Hells Gate, and Chasm. The Universe definitely has a sense of humor.

Eventually I stopped for the night in a city called Prince George, one of my guideposts with dad's name. A heavy rain had been falling for hours and remained as I pulled into town. Brake and headlights looked like a fireworks finale through the raindrops gathering on my windshield, red and white bursts in the dark, but the sleep-inducing back and forth of my wipers was bringing the day to a close. I spotted a station that looked open with a few semi's parked to one side of the lot, and was told by an employee it was alright to sleep there. The next morning I went inside to freshen up for the day.

"You're here all the way from Texas, eh?" the woman working said after seeing my license plates during the night. She offered me a free coffee and some fruit for the morning. Her kindness stilled whatever anxiety I had about being in a new place, a new country, all alone. Because in fact, I wasn't alone.

The rains of the previous day lifted to a drizzle. I opted against using my wipers and watched tiny drops gather, dancing and merging together on the windshield until they zoomed up and over my head, the force of the air moving around the car too great for them to hold on any longer. Each left a thin trail of water beads to prove their existence that would eventually grow, gather, and follow their lead.

The road I chose to drive through British Columbia had been stripped and was being relaid starting on the opposite side. Because of the recent rainfall everything was mud. All the cars around me looked like hell. Since Maude was white and rode low to the ground I was sure the mud mask she was getting would be fantastic. Motorcyclists had it the worst, splattered an inch thick in grime from head to toe. We all drudged on, migrating north to see the wonder of a world that's easiest to drive to during the few months of summer.

Signs to watch for wildlife were everywhere along roadsides. After spotting a handful of animals I rarely, if ever, saw, I started to make a list. I saw bears, bald eagles, a fox, mountain goats, a porcupine, caribou, moose that usually had a baby or two in tow, wild horses, and I actually had to stop and wait for a mama duck to cross with her line of ducklings behind her. I felt more in tune with nature as each creature made its appearance.

The longest day of the year was the following day. Even though I was outside my normal routine of going to bed and waking up with the sun, I wasn't. It was after midnight and still light out. It was such a surreal experience! I was driving on some rough two-lane roads through Yukon Territory in Northwestern Canada where the landscape and lighting were unlike any I had ever seen. While I enjoyed a mental game of trying to figure out what aperture, shutter speed, and film combination would best capture the moment, I kept my headlights on due to the caribou, moose, and other unidentifiable large animals that ran around enjoying the late night, or should I say early morning, sunshine. I was repeatedly startled when looking down at my speedometer, since it was switched to kilometers. *I'm going over 100! Oh wait.*

Maybe it was because I was so tired, but once I arrived at the travel plaza it looked straight out of a slasher flick. Colorful Christmas lights blinked unsteadily over old gas pumps, raggedy RV's were pulled into a camping area that wasn't well lit, a line of trucks sat humming with their lights set to dim on the other side, and there was a faint glow in the sky; still daylight at 2 AM. It was unnerving. I looked up where the next stop was. Nothing for hours. Admittedly, I was a little paranoid, but with no other option, I stayed. The woman at the register inside assured me that it was "perfectly safe." It ended up being fine. I was only nervous because it was different from any other place I had stayed at before.

The next morning, I blinked the sleep out of my eyes for a while rubbing my feet together, thankful they were warm. As I laid there staring at Maude's ceiling, my life didn't seem real. I would be in Alaska by noon that day. The fiftieth state I'd see in my lifetime!

I paid for a shower since it had been about a week since last washing my hair. The restaurant attached had WiFi so I decided to stay for breakfast and get in touch with the world; let people know I was still alive. As I waited for my breakfast of two eggs over medium and toast, I scrolled through days of emails and texts. The first, and only one, I read was a group message to my sister and I from our mom.

It began with, "Your father is ready to be picked up." How strange that sentence sounded in my head as I repeated it a few times. I said it out loud even though I was surrounded by other restaurant patrons.

"Your father is ready to be picked up," I said. Even more strange.

Dad donated his body to science. Whatever studies they had done were finished as of that week. His body was cremated sometime while I was driving through Canada. Mom wanted my sister and I to go with her to pick up his remains once I returned. While I was glad she asked and that I was included, my knees felt like they were knocked out from under me. Why did I have to receive such painful family news on such a big day for me personally? I regretted checking my phone.

Once my order came out, two eggs over easy with brown toast, I tried to finish my breakfast only thinking of what I was consuming; my first hot meal in I couldn't remember how long. Walking to my car, the news washed back over me. It had been comforting that he was still around. I liked to think he was just on an extended trip. Without a casket at the funeral I had somewhat fooled myself into believing that maybe he was still living.

I even called him once. Scrolling through the contacts on my phone until finding him, simply "Dad". Taking a deep breath, I hit call, not really sure why in that moment. In my mind I reasoned this was all just a big misunderstanding. He was actually somewhere exotic, and we couldn't get in touch with him because he had no signal. An elaborate story I'll admit.

After two rings and zero breaths, I hoped at least I could hear his voice on his voicemail. That would be a nice consolation I retreated, and better than nothing.

"Hello?" a man answered. I was in no way prepared for this.

"Oh hi," my voice unsteady over the lump in my throat. "Is... George there?"

"No, I'm sorry, you must have the wrong number," he replied. *No, I don't* was all I could think.

"I'm sorry too," I said finally. We awkwardly got off the phone and it sunk in a little deeper, the rouse I had created now dismantled. One more thing to deal with.

In reality, wherever his body was, he was helping people learn like he always wanted. He went back to school in a sense, an environment he excelled in, this time on the other side.

"He's ready to be picked up," was on repeat through my otherwise empty brain. Like I could just go drive and pick him up. Oh, what I would give to be able to go pick him up like we used to from work! He'd shuffle out to the car, throw his briefcase on the backseat, and plunk down in the passenger seat next to me.

"How was your day?" he'd ask in chipper fashion. That's one place I would drive forever to get to.

"He was *burned*. He's *ashes*. He's *gone!*" I cried.

The last stretch to Alaska was a tearful one. I felt broken, undone by the news I received from my mother. While I was away I could avoid thinking about the harsher realities of our situation. Her text made it impossible to run from the truth, no matter how far away I was.

The closer I got to the border my mood began to lift. *Enjoy the day you're in,* I reminded myself. I couldn't control the future, my grip on those reigns had been loosened long before. All I had was my car and the crazy bumpy road in front of me. Luckily, there was a lot of construction so my focus had to be on the drive, a welcome distraction.

Before the checkpoint to reenter the United States, which felt utterly bizarre since so many miles and days had passed between borders, a large wooden sign with golden letters inscribed across it greeted me on the left side of the road. "Alaska," was written in bold script lettering. The most splendid state sign of them all since it marked the last one in my life's collection. It was glorious!

As I entered the checkpoint, a big black raven welcomed me. Sitting on top of a security camera, about a foot away from my window and not moving an inch, he didn't look real. He finally let out a loud, "Caw!" that shook my calm space. He was announcing my arrival like a royal herald. Once I made it through the border, I looked at the countryside in front of me completely awestruck. A new piece of earth that many have never, and may never, see.

"Adventure!" I yelled, forging on. *"I DID IT! I drove to Alaska! I've seen every state of the United States of America!"*

I couldn't believe it. Some might call the year I had a mid-life crisis, but my life was in crisis before. I finally woke up. I was finally living!

A newly-paved silklike road glided beneath Maude through a landscape with little vegetation. A while into the drive an owl flew overhead to greet us. She was silhouetted against the clear sky just like a forest of trees now rapidly flying by on either side of the car. The white sun popped blindingly between their branches as it chased us on the other side; similar to my spirit, flashing brilliantly as it reignited.

Gradually the pavement began to move in gentle waves tossing my tiny vessel to and fro. The slight undulations rapidly became drastic and choppy. The harsh Alaskan winters had morphed the once level blacktop. There was no way I could keep up with the speed limit which was set at 65 miles per hour, poor Maude would fall apart! Old pickup trucks puttered along, their paint worn with rust spots around their wheel wells. They represented their home state with some of the first Alaskan license plates I had ever seen.

For a long while I sat behind an older man on a three-wheeled motorcycle with Florida plates. He had two small country flags waving in the wind behind him for the USA and Canada.

"That is awesome!" I said gleefully.

He and I rolled along weaving back and forth together, both of us in our victory lap and enjoying every second, trying to let the moment live as long as possible. Luminous poplar fluff floated through the high evening sun to help me envision what that place looked like in snow. I was there for the summer solstice. The day I entered Alaska was the longest day of the year. Something I hadn't planned, but all of the conditions and days serendipitously lined up to make it possible. In the region I was in, there would be twenty-one hours of daylight.

Perhaps it's a wives' tale, but one of my mom's friends used to say, "When the leaves on the trees turn over, it's going to rain."

As I drove through a grove of birch trees their leaves appeared to be flipped over, their underbellies shining lighter in color. It was bright and sunny apart from one lone dark cloud above. I wondered if her prediction would prove true. A few miles down the road the sky released as I drove through a sunshower; one of the most enlightening of phenomenons. The trees made me think of my dad and his late mother. He always said birch trees were her favorite, having planted some in the front yard at home.

In the hours that darkness fell I was unsure what was around the next turn and wished my headlights moved with the sharp snaking corners of the road instead of shining on the woods directly in front of me. Being cautious of wildlife, I was moving in slow motion as if driving through thick sludge. The night pressed in, crushing each side of my car as I tearfully slipped into nostalgia about how far away my old life was from the one I was driving through; a world away.

The next morning I woke up in the parking lot of the only gas station in miles, and gently set my intention for the day before even opening my eyes. With the extreme highs and lows of the previous day, it was a time to be kind to myself.

Bringing my palms together at heart center I proclaimed, "Love. Be love to myself today."

As I began to stretch I thanked my body for carrying me so far. It was healthy and dependable. Running my hands over my bare skin studying each hair that raised on my arms as I touched them, it occured to me what a miracle each one was!

That day I was conquering Denali National Park. When I first began my tour of the parks it became the coveted cherry on top. With the tallest mountain in the U.S. and it's peak geographic coordinates, it was the highest my adventure could take me.

"Oh, if it's possible, Lord, please help me get there," I prayed when marking it on my map with a star months before, and it was only minutes away!

When I arrived I was shaking, unable to pinpoint the feelings coursing through me. There were so many! Denali, my very own eyes were seeing it and my very own momentum got me there (with Maude's help of course). I felt like I needed to pinch myself. The drive there seemed eternal, dragging on and on through challenging roads for three grueling days and nights. A country once separated us, but no longer!

As I sat next to a bridge overlooking a stream I was on top of the world. Being the farthest north I had ever been, I truly was. I meditated and opened myself up to the possibility of future adventures. It wasn't the end of the road for me. I'd have more of them. I was sure of it.

My distant dreams of traveling abroad and seeing the world were shifting to reality. My fears of different languages, customs, and people wouldn't hold me back any longer. They didn't seem so scary anymore, and neither did going it alone. I was already doing it.

Nature's choir spoke to me as the sun heated my black jeans to burning. The sounds of a glassy brook eased my mind and body and her birds sang songs to embolden me. Life felt fluid and intensely real. In that moment, I fell in love with the precious life I was given. What a gift! My quest had recentered my inner compass. I finally found myself, my true north.

I watched a caribou while sitting there. She stood in the middle of a great valley and the entire scene was hers. She drank from fresh stream waters coming down off the mountains beyond, and then laid on the rocks to sun herself as I was. I pictured my spirit in her strong frame. With not a care in the world and no predators after her, she slept and I joined her. When I awoke she had moved on, like I would be soon. I said goodbye to my caribou friend at Denali, my spirit animal, promising her I'd continue to roam as she did.

That night I drove south to Anchorage for the best pizza that I was told to try, recommended by my new friends in Seattle. I ordered a pad thai pie, which was really tasty despite how it might sound. I often wish I could make the drive back just for that meal again. I'll go back one day. I still have to check off seeing the northern lights. The aurora borealis were on my bucket list before I knew the term. Looking at each place I visited, I promised them I'd be back.

My next destination was my hometown, the last place I wanted to be with our impending trip to "pick up Dad." At the same time, the day I planned to arrive we'd be celebrating Mom's sixtieth birthday, and I'm big on birthdays. My present? I would be driving over 4,000 miles to be with her.

I wanted to experience everyday rural areas in Alaska, not just what was off the highway, and explored roads I had a hard time finding on a map. One night I pulled into the only gas station in the area, but the line of cars at the pumps went on forever. Travelers hopped out and took their time milling around the store full of local wares and to and from the porta-potties across the parking lot. Each family seemed to have five or more people piling out of their vehicles.

"What is this, the circus!?" I fumed.

I thought I'd never get to the pump. According to my phone there was another gas station up the road. It hadn't been as accurate in the sticks, but I decided to take the chance. Who knows why I was in any rush. As I approached the spot allotted for the next station, a sinking feeling came over me. I was in the middle of a marshy wetland. How could there be a major gas station in a mile? As the feet counted down I realized my phone was wrong. Already almost an hour away from the last station, I figured surely there must be another one in an upcoming town.

I kept driving as I watched the miles vanish of what was left in Maude's tank. Not a town, not a house, nothing. I pulled to the side of the road to sit, think, and calculate the milage. If I kept driving I *might* find a gas station. Or was the safer choice to turn back and return to the one I left? In order to ensure that I wouldn't run out of gas, turning back was unfortunately the best and only option. I scolded myself for the first ten minutes heading back to where I started.

"If I would've waited a few more minutes I could have saved myself more than two extra hours of driving time!" I complained.

A whisper came through my window on the wind. *"Patience,"* it said gently.

The path ahead came to a single lane construction area with a stoplight, meaning cars were coming through in the opposite direction. I took a few deep breaths while waiting. Soon the six or seven cars I had been behind at the pump earlier rolled by on their way forward. I wanted to hide, sink down in my seat and slide out from under my car... but there was no escaping. Once the light turned green, I began the drive repeating *"patience"* out loud to myself. I took my time once getting back, no one else there but me.

Going against the grain of my usual patterns, I slept at rest stops throughout the state. I had only stayed at one prior to my time there while traveling in the eastern portion of the lower forth-eight in the wee hours of the morning, can't even recall the location. Despite my hesitation, being the only car in the parking lot, I stayed too worn out to continue. When I awoke a dozen other cars were also parked, their drivers all snoozing. Rest areas usually felt too secluded to me. I was more comfortable around other people and cars under bright lights. Truck stops were my safety in the night offering greater security and most of the comforts of home.

Alaskan rest areas were very quiet. Since I had been trying to stay up with the sun, I reached the point of delirium and had to stop. With only one or two cars and campers in each lot, I asked for an extra layer of protection to surround my car as I floated between thoughts and sleep.

"What is that!?" I exclaimed as I saw my first glacier the next morning. That certainly was a surprise I didn't think I'd be seeing! The faint blue formations were arresting. They reminded me of one of my questions to dad in his final weeks, this one a common youthful inquiry.

"Dad, what's your favorite color?" I asked. His green eyes looked around the room a minute and met mine again. At this point he wasn't able to move much, but he squeezed my hand as I held his.

"Blue. But not just any old blue. Not blue with a little bit of white in it. White with a little bit of blue in it," he said. I found the color he was describing. It was glacier blue.

Oh, how my soul would miss Alaska, that otherworldly place, with its extraordinary sights and captivating sunsets that stretched on for hours with the same glow in the sky from 10 PM to 2 AM, a baffling light source that grew on me while I was there. What was I going to do upon returning back to normal time?

When I reemerged through the Canadian border, I felt new. I battled some of my darkest and scariest demons during those long days of sun and felt the grip of darkness that had settled over me releasing. Moving through the crisp air with a newfound courage, no longer sludgy, I felt light and fast heading toward my future.

After multiple recommendations to see Liard River Hot Springs from people I met across Canada, it became my next destination. On the way I stopped at a gas station before they closed. They had a full grocery store attached so I was able to pick up produce for the upcoming days. As I browsed, the cashier asked where I was headed and I told him.

"Be careful of the buffalo this time of night!" he warned me.

"Oh sure, OK," I scoffed after many a sarcastic encounter like this one.

"No, I'm serious. There are buffalo everywhere on the next stretch of road. Be careful!" he stressed.

For the most part, I've let go of the totally gullible side of myself that immediately says, "Oh really!?" as my knee-jerk reaction. I thanked him for the heads-up and was on my way. *How weird*, I thought as I got in my car.

A few miles down the highway there were huge bright yellow flashing signs across the top of the roadway that read, "BEWARE OF BUFFALO." I laughed out loud, thoroughly dumbfounded. Dark slow-moving shadowy icebergs that were definitely far larger than my vehicle were everywhere! Since everyone else apparently knew not to drive at dusk in that area I was the only car for miles. I turned on my high beams and drove cautiously down a minefield of countless buffalo! It was, by far, one of the craziest hours of my life.

Since the drive through them took up more time than anticipated, I arrived to town later than expected. The parking lot of a lodge next to a line of trucks seemed like the best place to roll out my car camping set up for the night. In the morning I got ready in the car and went in to see what they had for breakfast. As I waited for a sandwich to go, I looked at a wall of photographs about when the hot springs were discovered and the construction of the walkway that led to it.

"I thought they found the springs when they put the highway in," a man said next to me as he looked at the display.

His dad helped build the Alaska Highway that we were traveling on. He came up with his dad and son for the 50th Anniversary of the highway's completion. When I met him he and his daughter were there to celebrate the 75th Anniversary, celebrating his father's life together. I told him I was on a solo trip, in a way celebrating my dad, to Alaska and back from the lower forty-eight. I hadn't driven the highway up but was driving the entire length of it back.

"Well, life is short. Do it while you can. I think it's great that you're going for it by yourself," he told me. He spoke about how fleeting life can be, sharing that his wife had passed away suddenly. Watching her go was one of the hardest things he had ever been through. He drifted for a moment. I silently stood with him, holding space for her memory as he went to a place far away, thinking of her. When he snapped to he looked at me expectantly.

"That's why I'm on this trip," I replied. "My dad passed away last year. I'm sure he would have loved to do something like this. It's really neat how you're making these memories with your daughter." He gave me a warm smile and a fatherly pep talk about safety on the road. Talking with him felt like a morning blessing; a talk with Dad.

The long boardwalk I read about led to the springs over a shallow swampy area. It was a slender wooden deck raised about a foot off the water, just wide enough for two people to pass each other going in opposite directions. Families went in and out like breaths in single file lines. I took off my shoes at the start and let myself sink into a walking meditation, mindfully awakening each of my senses. I straightened my back and posture concentrating on each movement as I envisioned a string pulling me up through the crown of my head to the sky above.

Steam began billowing from behind a hut up ahead. I walked through the bathhouse to see a spacious clear lagoon where other bathers sat in a foggy mist that appeared to lift them up. Their rosy complexions made them look like cherubs sitting in the clouds. Oversized leaves and other greenery hung over the sides of the water: a secluded tropical hideaway in the middle of Canada!

"Whoa!" I exclaimed as my body parted the water's surface. "It's going to be cold getting out of here!"

The surrounding bathers laughed softly. Soon my thoughts slowed down to match theirs as my skin absorbed the warmth, sending goosebumps down my arms and legs. I began to release any and all bad energy that my aching body had been lugging around. The heat felt incredible as I submerged my head, each hair follicle coming alive, tingling one by one.

I got in near two women that were about my age. They were also heading southbound from Alaska on a joyride together, moving one of them down to Oregon. They asked what brought me up that way.

"Well, once I finalized my divorce, my dad passed away shortly afterward," I told them. "The one-two punch kinda knocked me out. I went through a bit of a breakdown, honestly, and decided to hit the open road to get away from it all."

"Oh my gosh!" one of them replied. "We've both lost our dads," as she motioned to her friend sitting next to her. "I lost my dad four years ago and she just lost her dad…"

"In April," her friend added.

As I looked back and forth between them I realized they were my bookends. One had been dealing with her loss for a while longer and the other's was fresher than mine, not even three months. We were all in different stages of our grief.

"I know we're in our swimsuits, but is it ok if I hug you?" I asked the woman who had just lost her dad months earlier. She teared up as she nodded yes.

The three of us talked for what felt like an hour. We were connected through the loss of our dads and became an instant support to one another. We covered everything from the day it happened, to the change in family dynamics once our fathers were gone, dividing their belongings between our mothers and siblings, selling the family home, relationships we've had since, and our own personal journeys of growth through it all.

I had lived and relived my saga so many times, I just wanted to listen and let their stories take over for a while. As I absorbed the power of the water up to my neck, I let my mouth go quiet. What were they feeling? What could I learn from them? There were days I felt so isolated in my story, and then I'd meet fellow travelers like them that were going through the same things I was. Hot springs are said to be a sacred place of healing, and my experience that day was no exception. That visit went an incredibly long way in mending both my body and my heart.

After a couple of hours on the road, I came around a corner to see a herd of mountain goats across the highway. My quick turn of the wheel to dodge them sent a sharp pain down my back, so I found a quiet spot to pull off and rest a while. The constant strain from sitting in the same position for hours on end called for regular breaks anyway.

A bed of flowers carpeted the ground with black and yellow butterflies floating between them. A great drop-off curved around where I sat with a rushing river flowing at the bottom of it. As I looked at hills that skimmed the skyline, I decided the moment called for a mini yoga session. In recent months I had gotten used to practicing anywhere since my "home practice" was everywhere—town parks, campsites, the beach—no matter. I actually found I loved meditation and yoga even more outdoors with the container of a room removed. The air invigorated my wild bones as I breathed it all in deeply, my motions strong and deliberate.

Later in the day I came across a group of cars gathered beside the freeway with tourists leaping across in front of me like gazelles. Either an accident or, most likely, another animal sighting. I never quite understood the allure of getting out of a vehicle when seeing a large animal. It produced the opposite reaction in me. Everyone's camera lenses and binoculars were pointed at the tree line. As I rolled by my assumption was confirmed, a family of bears was up in the branches of a tree.

"No way, driving on by jokers! That's terrifying!" I laughed. I'm more of a "keep your arms and legs inside the vehicle while passing large animals that are really close to the road and could charge at any minute" type of person.

My ex and I saw a family of bears like that in Great Smoky Mountains National Park in the eastern portion of Tennessee once. Tourists were out of their cars taking pictures and then all of a sudden the bears began to make their way down the trunks of the trees they were in, and those dudes are fast! Alarm quickly spread through the crowd as everyone ran to the safety of their cars (including us).

Still in what would have been our tenth year of marriage, although divorced, I saw my next stop as that anniversary trip most couples plan. Banff National Park, my first Canadian National Park! It was near where we went on our honeymoon. I wondered what he was doing that day, if he could sense that I returned there, or if he had gone through any portion of the emotional journey I had. With everything in me, I hoped to leave my heartache and dashed dreams there. Like newlyweds with cans affixed to their bumper, the broken parts of me were along for the ride, too. That park was a very big place, big enough to hold all of it. I'd still feel it on occasion, but I intended on leaving the bulk of my pain behind.

"I'm shouting to the mountains! I'm leaving him here!" I yelled out my window. In a more somber tone I pleaded, *"Please, take it."*

I stopped to ask park employees if they recommended any side roads apart from the main freeway, hoping to see as much Canadian wilderness as possible before crossing back into the states. I did this often to escape major interstates, especially if I had already taken them. Taking local roads through small towns in New England and adventuring west on Historic Route 66 instead of the turnpikes and tollways that replaced them was more fun. They recommended I take an alternate route that skirted through the country and eventually dumped back into major interstate. It would add a bit of time to the drive, but I was up for the adventure.

Upon entering the welcome lodge, the smell of chicken, pretzels, and other hot foods drew me in. Hunger pulled me across the room like a cartoon character that floats through the air on a scent. I was down to half a can of lima beans, black beans, and a tin of almonds in the car. Since the cheapest selection was a small popcorn that was my splurge, my version of living large while on a shoestring budget.

I drove toward the hiking trails on Icefields Parkway with the unimaginable Canadian Rockies towering all around me. As I pulled out my bag of hot popcorn for breakfast, I was suddenly an active participant in my own nature documentary. Usually made with sweeping shots from a helicopter or airplane, this movie was made with my car. My windshield became a rectangular screen with a motion picture of mountains and lakes I had never seen before. There I was eating my popcorn, enjoying the show.

The trail at Mistaya Canyon crossed a bridge over a raging river between massive rounded boulders that were layered thinly, like they were made from the drips of candle wax. I stood on the bridge mesmerized by the water's gushing swirls like the ever-changing flames of a campfire. Each one sanded down another invisible layer of the rocks they moved through, having been polished smooth through the tumbling years of its flow. That place felt sacred; like an altar to the marvels of the earth.

I followed the bridge to a path on the other side and planted myself there, sitting on one of the boulders at the edge of the water. My gaze followed the river upstream between soaring slender pines to jagged snow-capped mountains that pointed onward, up toward a white infinite sky. The world felt limitless! I never wanted to leave. I wanted to build a house right in that very spot to see that view and have that feeling everyday for the rest of my life.

Next was Peyto Lake, known as fox lake since it's shaped like one. It's glacier-fed and such a brilliant shade of turquoise it looks unreal. It was one of those moments where I felt the need to rub my eyes. Was I really seeing what I was seeing!?

Walking back to my car over a sloping trail, I was behind a couple that reminded me of my parents. The man in the sage green shirt, dad jeans, and white tennis shoes had no clue he was a stand-in for someone dearly departed. I enjoyed walking behind them, pretending it really was my mom and dad. I followed them like my sister and I did on every family trip we took growing up. I wanted to call out, "Wait for me!" as I skipped towards them.

When late afternoon ushered in I decided to pack up and hit the scenic route I was told about. Breaking away from the highway, the view started to look familiar for the first time in weeks. An initial dismay, then dread, turned to panic as I realized it might be the same way we drove together on our honeymoon all those years before. Once I was certain that it was the same road I pulled over, my vital organs temporarily forgetting how to function. I considered turning around. What emotions was I stirring up? *Was this a good idea?*

The repeating click of Maude's emergency flashers brought me back to the present like a metronome steadying my heart. There was a stone corridor that the road disappeared around up ahead. Like my life, I didn't know what was around the next bend, but decided to press on anyway.

I pictured a rich velvet stage curtain rising while driving through it. My life could be whatever I wanted it to be. I didn't see that future for myself all those years before, but was so glad to be unattached driving through the second time around.

I passed restaurants, coffee shops, and artisan stands we visited together on our honeymoon, and even pulled into the resort where we stayed. But the once pristine white buildings were dingy and sagging. Mold grew up the siding, bikes were chained to porches, and broken-down cars sat in the parking lot; the complex had been turned into cheap apartments. I saw my weathered marriage in the decay that had taken over. Changed forever.

Following the Rocky Mountains down through the border of Montana, I felt each mile on the soles of my feet, up through my ankles, and rumbling through to my calves. Having driven so much I knew they would be swollen the next day. With my speed set to cruise, I'd lift them up one at a time to try and give them a break.

The look of the road at night soothed my aches. Reflectors lined the broken white lines and guardrails transforming my path into an airport runway. Towering semi trucks flashed their brights at me to remind me to turn mine to dim, the blinking taillights of another thanked me for letting him pass as I signaled back "you're welcome," with two flashes of my headlights, and gusts of air jostled my car in brief torrents as they closely passed in the opposite direction. No longer solo drivers humming by one another, they were my friends, my community out on the road. Now schooled in driving etiquette, I enjoyed talking to other solo drivers this way. That evening I pined for a spot in the parking lots of motels while quietly passing by in the dark, but like so many nights before, couldn't afford a room no matter how tired I was.

The next day's adventure was Glacier National Park in northern Montana. Half of the park was closed due to snow and road construction, but the part I saw was beginning to see signs of spring with purple, blue, and white flowers blanketing the ground. At an overlook for Saint Mary Lake with mountains on all sides, I stood there thinking about how seeing new landscapes makes me feel. It's truly a spiritual experience, which was underscored given the lake's name. I believed in a deeper way upon viewing each grand vista, like another feature of God's face had been revealed. How could something so unbelievable be real? Well there it was, as real as real can be.

That evening the world turned into a luscious Impressionist painting. Wavy hills along the roadside looked like giant curtains blowing in the wind, highlands were hemmed in by bands of grey rain to my left, and on my right, flattened plains stretched out under a sky in every color on an artists' palette. I was driving through a living, breathing, masterpiece! It was a moving pastel dream.

After crossing into Wyoming, I drove by a small town park with baseball diamonds aglow from bright lights that turned the night to day. Kids threw the ball around practicing on some fields, games were in play with everyone in uniform on others, and families watched and cheered from the stands all around. Many evenings of my childhood looked just like that, only a few states away.

It felt like so much of the country I had already driven through. It could have been New Hampshire, Wisconsin, Mississippi; anyplace, really. I drove past incalculable lives every day. I went by all kinds of homes with families playing and working together in their yards. Row houses, starter homes, brownstones, apartments, painted ladies, and trailers—there were many types of homesteads. Little plots of land that people were caretakers of. Homes are a bit like animal burrows where each person can retreat to safety; their shelter from the storm.

There were factories and mills in production, strip malls housing various stores and offices, diners filled with teenagers, and seniors enjoying their discounted morning coffee with old friends. Then there was the newer side of America that was much different from those generations before with its rows of vacant storefronts, boarded up chain restaurants, and warehouses long since forgotten. Everything was familiar even though I had never been there before. As I went by I imagined living in each place, and wondered if I'd be a different person if given a new set of circumstances. After so much time on the road, I was beginning to realize every place was kind of the same.

I broke into a private karaoke session as I drove that night singing power ballads with musical legends on the radio. Songs like *What's Love Got To Do With It* by Tina Turner and *I Hate Myself For Loving You* by Joan Jett & The Blackhearts rattled my windows as I maxed out my speakers. I sang each familiar melody with reckless abandon, dancing my heart out.

"Yeah! That's exactly how I feel!" I shouted back to the speakers.

Something aligned in me that night more than any other time I previously heard those songs. I felt supported by them, understood. I tried to match the volume of the music with my voice as I belted lyrics about love and loss. I was overcoming my fear of being alone and felt more empowered with every note.

I woke up in the Black Hills of South Dakota to forceful winds abrasively lashing about my car. The large florescent sign for the gas station and restaurant I parked at overnight clanged and banged overhead, becoming my alarm for the morning. I felt seasick as Maude shook back and forth, fighting to stay upright. As we drove, she battled against harsh side winds that roared off open fields. With each large vehicle that passed I'd get a small reprieve, making use of their wall of protection. As they cleared my car a sudden burst of wind blew so fierce it almost knocked me off the side of the road. My arms and shoulders were tense as they attempted to control the steering wheel.

After making a stop through Wall Drug for their famous 5-cent cup of coffee, I arrived at Badlands National Park in the western portion of South Dakota and sat for a while in a line of cars at the entrance. I took comfort in the large American flag waving proudly above me in the strong wind at the Ranger Station. I had returned to my own country from my voyage beyond. I wrestled with the road and myself during the longest solo, and this time international, expedition I had been on to date. On the other side of it, discovering something new in a framework that was familiar; it felt so good to be back.

home

I skated across the Clark Bridge over the mighty Mississippi where it connects Missouri to my hometown at 5 AM on Mom's sixtieth birthday. The sun crested over the curve of the earth in red at the horizon, morphing to peach, baby blue, navy, to black. Long banded smears ran parallel to the road on my windshield; my handiwork when I attempted to wash and squeegee the windows at the last stop. Bug splatters came alive in sleepy waves, glowing as I passed under each street lamp.

"I'm baaack," I sang in a whisper. The familiar yellow-coated cables of the bridge greeted me with wide welcoming arms once more.

We celebrated mom with a family visit at the petting zoo. She rode the merry-go-round with the grandkids, fed baby goats, and rode the kiddie train through the park with the whole family to look at longhorns and llamas. It was her first birthday without dad since she was nineteen. After forty years together, it was the first with no flowers, card, dinner, or kiss. We tried our best to make her big milestone memorable, but we all knew what would overshadow the memory of the day: that he was missing from it.

The next morning the sky moaned as she, my sister, and I drove to St. Louis. Since I was in town, we were going to pick up Dad. None of us said much during the hour drive there. When we pulled into the parking lot of the crematory we turned off the car and sat, staring blankly, as the sky let loose in sheets of rain around the car. We all turned toward each other at the same moment as if our family DNA aligned perfectly for a millisecond, "I'm not ready for this," being the general consensus. We talked about him and the things we were starting to forget, all helping each other remember.

We longed to hear his voice again, and my sister remembered she had the only surviving voicemail on her phone.

"Want me to play it?" she asked after finding it. Both Mom and I nodded.

"Hey, this is Dad," he said. "We'll be pulling in here soon. Take your time and get here safely. We'll be inside. We're going to sit over by the musicians again. Maybe go a few rows up. Anyway, we'll see you soon. Bye."

Our parents were pulling into the parking lot at church. He was letting my sister know where she could find them once they got there. Not even a minute long, it was one of those everyday exchanges we so wished to have back again. Although his voice was different, as everyone's is on voicemail, I realized I had almost forgotten what he sounded like. An idea or memory of his voice was so different than actually hearing it.

We all breathed a deep sigh after passing the box of tissues around and decided to make a run for it. The three of us hopped out of the car and ran towards an awning covering the sidewalk to escape the deluge. Before entering we paused to hold hands, the three of us linked like a chain, rang the doorbell, and opened the door as we were buzzed in. A man asked who we were there for and mom replied with his full name. This was repeated three times between them, a deep and sudden twinge twisting into my lower spine with each one. Our last time hearing it was at his funeral.

Eventually, a woman emerged with a large white shopping bag like you get at a department store. My eyes followed it through the air, landing on my sister's expression as the bag was placed on the counter a few inches from her face with a thud. I'm sure all three of us stared at that woman just as blankly as we had upon our arrival out in the car. Once papers were signed the three of us peered over the lip of the bag. A black plastic box smaller than a shoebox.

"Can we sit down a minute?" I asked feeling lightheaded. The girls looked pretty green, too.

"Now what do we do?" one of us finally asked.

"Where would Dad want to go?" asked another.

"Home," we all said together.

We got out to the car and couldn't see him sitting on the backseat or floorboard, so we buckled the white bag into the passenger seat of the car he purchased. Most of the time they had that vehicle he was too sick to drive, so that was always his seat. I even turned on the seat heater for him, his favorite feature. My sister and I both piled in the back. Mom looked at us, then at him.

"Okay," she said through tears, her lips quivering. "Let's go home."

Once we got there we went about finding a special bottle of red wine from the pantry. Mom and Dad ordered a case of it when they were out in Napa Valley on the West Coast the year before. Requiring time to age, it would be shipped at a later date. The box arrived a few months after he passed away, so he never got the chance to enjoy it.

Mom and I tearfully cracked the first bottle open on their thirty-sixth wedding anniversary, their first one apart. We drank it out of the matching silver goblets they used at their wedding reception, which had been proudly on display in her china cabinet as long as I could remember. She saved the remaining bottles for special occasions like holidays and his birthday. This was definitely one of those times.

When we opened the black box inside the white bag, it contained a clear plastic bag of his ashes with a tiny hospital bracelet with his name printed on it stapled to the top. My sister removed it from the box and sat cradling his ashes like a newborn baby, big crocodile tears slowly streaming down her cheeks. The sound was so familiar from our childhood, as if she had scraped her knee; an unrelenting breathy cry.

Before he died, Dad told us he wanted his ashes scattered on the bluffs of The Great River Road near their home.

"I want to fly with the eagles!" he told us.

Bald eagles returned to the area every year during the coldest winter months. In Dad's last years he and Mom photographed them on that road which ran between the river and the bluffs. They would leave an hour earlier than they needed to so they could stop to take pictures on their way into town. He'd hop out on the side of that busy road with his chemo pack slung over his shoulder and run across traffic to get the best angle. Something about their power and grace called to him. Still coming to terms with what we had in our hands, we decided to hold off. Mom wanted to keep him with her for a while.

I began preparing for my next adventure, the heaviness of that day giving me the jitters. My legs were jumpy like they could run forever and I was homesick for the road. I drove northbound on I-35 to Minnesota, a drive we took often to see Mom's side of the family in the Twin Cities growing up. We would spend summers at the lake, visited for holidays, and celebrated birthdays with our entire extended family. It was my second time that year to make the trip to Minneapolis by myself, which I had never done before.

I passed red-tailed hawks on telephone poles that dad would be trying to capture with his camera and patchwork quilt fields of corn and soybeans that reminded me of mom's talent with a needle and thread. The notion that, "all roads are connected," crossed my mind when I saw a sign for Austin, Minnesota. I lived off of I-35 for years in Austin, Texas and filed away a rainy day trip, making the drive from Austin to Austin, south on 35 from the state where I was born to the place I was reborn.

My visit was during the week of Fourth of July and my family rearranged their schedules to make special plans while I was in town. We spent those summer nights barbecuing at the drive-in movie theater, my cousins and I rode a neon ferris wheel together, we went on a bike ride to see the local fireworks show, I jumped off the high dive at the lake with my cousin's kids, and we made root beer floats at grandma and grandpa's house.

The last of which was one of the most major feats in mending relationships my entire trip. A reunion with my grandma, who due to a family storyline outside of my own, I hadn't seen in almost two decades. We sat around my grandma and grandpa's dining room table like nothing had ever happened, the only difference being we had all aged quite a lot. I finally returned to the motherland and found forgiveness in my heart for any distance that had come between us.

There were a few friends I had similar experiences with on my journey, finally coming to an understanding of why we lost touch, but this one was the most central to my healing. I was able to revisit and confront my inner child for a wound that was never mine to carry. One that was impossible to heal without seeing her again. I melted like butter as she wrapped her arms around me in a hug, one of the best feelings I've ever experienced.

My aunt was in an Independence Day parade while I was in town. I didn't know a soul in the crowd, but it was just like anywhere else; Main Street USA. Cheerleaders danced by with pompoms fluttering, marching bands played in formation, firetrucks drove by with kids waving from the front seat, signs for congressmen and folks vying for local offices adorned floats, an oversized grocery cart was pulled by a tractor advertising their local market, beauty queens rode in the back of convertibles or "princesses" as I heard a daddy tell his daughter, and candy and beads were thrown out to children in the front row.

I was beaming! I could have been standing anywhere in America. Throughout the previous year, everywhere across the country felt like home at one time or another. The red, white, and blue decorations on parade floats, people's clothing, and hundreds of flags blowing in the wind spoke to me. It was a grand celebration of my homeland and year.

Being in Minnesota was a walk through my past that I never wanted to end. Yet, once the holiday passed and family needed to get back to their lives, I moved on. As I drove west a huge booming storm cloud chased me into a pure amber sunset. Ponds and lakes reflected the same color while all other land masses grew dark and sinister. The violet clouds cracked and flashed in charged bursts, lightning occasionally pulsing like a tangle of veins branching across the sky, never touching down.

My next stop was Theodore Roosevelt National Park off of Highway 94 in North Dakota where the landscape is picturesque, each view resembling American paintings and drawings lining walls in museums. Many of the viewpoints stood high above the ground which lended to this flattened quality. The earth appeared to end at a certain point, like the land and sky merged together on one plane. Dark green bushes and shrubs speckled the pale yellow grasses like spots on an eggshell.

As I crept along I saw my first prairie dogs in the wild. Hundreds of them popped up out of their holes in the ground, sitting tall and proud on their hind legs next to their homes. They appeared to be on the lookout. The squeaks and squawks they made to one another were so curious; a diverse code language amongst themselves. Feral horses wandered free without branding or saddles. One stood high above me on a hill and looked down as if it were a statue, hardly moving a muscle. I saw him as the keeper of the land, kind of like those lion statues that sit on stately porches or flank entrances to important buildings.

Now more comfortable with them, I parked at a rest stop in Montana to sleep that night. In the morning I walked down to the shore of the Yellowstone River, where I sat by the night before, noticing the swiftness of its current in the daylight. The mosquitos had quickly scared me away my first visit. As I sat for a quiet moment my heartbeat began to sync with the river, feeling softer and more willing to accept all that I would see in the upcoming days. Something was beginning to shift inside of me.

Getting back in the car and starting the drive again a thought came to me, "Here I am, having the time of my life!" Forget about the sad days, I mean, of course there were those. The inner torment, *"Nothing seems to be going right anymore!"* Sometimes my thoughts would wind up on a loop of problems, things I needed to do, or fantasizing about this man or that. It could get tricky being in a quiet car alone for hours on end. The mind can go to crazy places creating fictional storylines since the material to construct mental movies is endless!

Letting my thoughts run away with me made everything that was physical and literal go fuzzy. Not that I wasn't paying attention to the road, but holy moly... I was in Yellowstone country! There were huge mountains all around and a sky wider than I had ever seen! There was a lot more to think about and live for than dwelling on things that were unpleasant or that were based on future events which might never happen at all.

Upon entering Yellowstone National Park from Gardiner, Montana, I came across a sign that I had to double back to re-read. "45th Parallel of Latitude Halfway Between Equator and North Pole." All at once, I felt the world grow smaller, holding me from all sides. Those faraway places weren't so far off after all.

Dawn was breaking over the plateau and the animals were cold and lazy with sleep like me. An elk came up close to say hello. Had I put my hand out I could have touched him, giving me the feeling of being warmly greeted by the place.

"Hi baby, aren't you pretty?" I said sweetly.

At my first stop I gazed intently at steaming water flowing over white sudsy rocks that looked like large oval bricks of salt. It felt like I was on another planet! I stopped at Frying Pan Spring, which sounded like bacon sizzling on the stovetop, the smell not so pleasant. The earth bubbled, boiled, and popped while funnel clouds of steam twisted toward the sky like mini tornados. Cracks in the ground became cloud machines as gases filled the air everywhere! I bounded up stairways and walked swiftly down wooden paths finding an energy I wasn't expecting. I felt my own force, my steps loud and cumbersome. I was pounding the hurt and anger out with each step, letting off steam with my surroundings.

Finding a quiet spot to splash in a stream when the midday heat turned up, I escaped the crowd. It's still possible to steal a private moment away, even in a tourist destination like Yellowstone. By the edge of the water I took my shoes off to ground myself. I was everywhere in the world all at once in that one tiny corner of it and begged the sun not to leave as it began to cross the sky. I wanted that golden moment to stay as it was forever.

"Maybe one day I'll live near a stream, so I can lay next to her waters anytime I like," I thought as I submerged my hands and feet at the shoreline. "Yes, I'd like that."

A family pulled up, parked in the only space behind me, and two teenage girls jumped out, one with short blonde hair, the other with long brown hair. They looked like my sister and I when we were young. The girls made a beeline for the water while the couple accompanying them took pictures. It was like watching my own family in another lifetime.

Miss Robin also came to visit me there. She made the long trip, too! I imagined she was the same one I saw making her summer nest on the beach at Olympic National Park in Washington. She had homes everywhere like me. She was courageous and I felt the same seeing her again. If she could weather the skies of those different places, so could I.

As the day stretched on I continued to amble down trails in an alien world of geysers, surreal land formations, and overwhelming smells all in a wide spectrum of deep rich colors. Everywhere I looked there were vapors rising from layers of filmy rocks and mud that oozed and crackled. I could feel the heat emitting from them as I passed by, curing me while dancing through their veils of smoke. No wonder it was the world's very first national park, making it a protected area. I spent an entire day seeing and experiencing things that were 100% new.

As I stared with my mouth agape at the edge of Grand Prismatic Spring, I couldn't believe what I was seeing. The colorful layers revealed below the surface within that hot acidic pool were more brilliant than any rainbow I had ever seen! I didn't even notice the Park Ranger that came and stood next to me.

"Astounding isn't it!?" she said in sheer wonderment. I looked around, she was talking to me.

"Yes. It has me in a trance," I told her.

"I remember my first time seeing these things," she said. "I still get the same feeling, it doesn't matter how many times you see it!"

As I was leaving the park that evening a torrential rain caused parkgoers to scurry to their cars or other shelter. With the wet conditions and road construction, traffic came to a standstill.

As I sat there I saw a family running to their car to escape the rain—my eyes glued to what looked like the father figure. He was trying to keep up with his family, one hand bracing his stomach, the other outstretched in front reaching for them. He came to a stop and put his hands on his head as the raindrops pelted his face. As he did so I could see his ostomy bag peek from under his pale yellow shirt. The same bulge Dad had the last year or so of his life. There he was again. Too tired and worn out to keep up with the rest of us, he was separated from the pack, standing alone in the rain. Up the road a bit, I pulled the car off to the shoulder and cried as hard as the rain that fell around me.

A few days later I crossed into Idaho to arrive at Craters of the Moon National Monument and Preserve. When I found that place while thumbing through my atlas, I knew I couldn't miss it, given its name. Even though a new piece of my loss most likely awaited me, I went there to face it.

I got out of my car at high noon in their parking lot, and felt as if I stepped onto the surface of the sun instead of the moon. Sweat ran down my legs instantly as I stood up. When I turned around I noticed the seat of my car had a perfect damp outline of the contours of my body. I opted for no air conditioner most days to be easier on Maude and so I'd be better acclimated to hike long distances. Heat swelled in bands over the road across the blackened bare land ahead. I grabbed the lightest dress in my collection for a quick change.

The edge of each narrow pathway sloped down on both sides and I was careful to walk right down the middle. It seemed like an extremely menacing place, even more so than any desert I had visited. I was a tiny timid mortal walking somberly through towering structures of lava and past burnt up dead looking trees. *If I were to stumble off course, would anyone find me?*

A family at the top of Inferno Cone looked like tiny dots in a row where the land and sky finally met at the horizon. I began to make my way up the long blackened hillside of tiny pebbly lava towards them, thankful that another family recommended sturdier shoes in the parking lot. Sandals would not have sufficed. Each step crunched beneath my boots like nails on a chalkboard; an unsettling sensation that I had to get past if I was going to make it the whole way.

When I made it to the top, there was one lone large tree that I sat under. The roots that protruded from the ground at its base were wide and wavy like smooth arms. Mama Earth embraced me as I rested, hugging my shape perfectly whether sitting or lying down. I spent time catching my breath and letting my sweat cool as a breeze came to visit, the cloak of her heavy branches covering me from the heat of the day.

As I began the walk back to the car I noticed two large rocks a few feet from each other. Standing between them, the love I still had for my dad and my ex overwhelmed me. It was an invasive, ferocious, unwanted half the time, killed me on the inside, never-ending, eternal kind of love that just ached deep down in my soul. The conflicting emotions surrounding my ex began to flow over as I cried because I still, even after everything, loved him, while sometimes hating him at the same time. I wanted to remember the good times, not just the bad. What about the love? Where did it go? Where could it go?

"It was never my intention to harm either of you in any way," I said aloud. "I'm sorry for the times that I did. I'm leaving the pain we caused one another here. I don't want to carry those burdens anymore. They're too heavy. Thank you for everything you gave me in this lifetime, for loving me, and for being a part of my journey." I kissed my fingers and held my hand to each stone sending an energy of love to both of them, then made the walk back down the hill.

That evening I stopped at a rest area on my way to see Grand Teton National Park which sits just south of Yellowstone in Wyoming. It was quiet with no other vehicles in the parking lot when I arrived. I prepared for bed in the bathroom as usual and then sat down at an outdoor table to read for a while and enjoy the sunset. A few cars full of people pulled in for a restroom break. Laughing loudly and carrying on, all of a sudden I felt vulnerable, outnumbered, and unsafe for one of the first times while traveling alone.

I took a little walk down to an overlook to watch the sunset over a creek bed and invited a sense of ease back in. When I turned around I began to weep—a wide rainbow stretched across the mountains in the direction I would be heading the following morning. My reminder that I was going the right way. No need to worry, I was taken care of.

Darkness ushered in sleep early that evening, even though I was soaring on excitement for the following day. I wanted to visit the Tetons on the trip out west with my ex the summer before we split. We arrived in Yellowstone late in the day so he decided we wouldn't have time to see the Tetons, a place I had always wanted to go. When my solo road trip began I decided to make whatever sacrifice necessary; I would be seeing those mountains. That's why it became one of my top 5 destinations in my wonders of America. I had already checked off most of them, and this was one of the biggest. It was a personal point of redirection.

Taking my time driving there the next morning, my heart pounded in my chest louder than the bass of the music playing, so I turned it off and pulled to the side of the road. Stepping out of the car, I sat on Maude's hood for a while, looking at the path of possibilities before me. I got down and sat at the edge of the gravel shoulder to run my hands through a cluster of velvety foxtails.

"Magic, remember the magic," I reminded myself as my wooden sparrow ring flew across the surface of the soft tans and greens of nature.

It was my placeholder ring, the one I put on the day I took off my wedding ring. A friend gave it to me eons before but it broke soon after. My sister fixed it the day I decided to stop wearing my wedding ring. She superglued and clamped the wooden piece back onto the metal frame it sat in.

"You're a free bird!" she told me as she put it on my left ring finger.

Whenever I'd forget to wear it my fingers would move to adjust my wedding ring like I had for years, now only a phantom ring. So for the first few years after my divorce I wore my replacement every single day.

I hopped across the freeway with not a car in sight in either direction and took a picture of Maude to document the moment before achieving my dream. Her body was covered in dirt and grime like mine. We came through a lot to get there. I felt such an overwhelming sense of fulfillment once those peaks finally came into view.

"I made it here all by myself!" I shouted out the window.

At first sight of them I got out of the car and a small white butterfly grazed my arm to welcome me. In a nearby tree I noticed Miss Robin, too. She made the trip to join me again! Cloud-looking blossoms appeared as big as the snow caps on the mountain ridge behind them from my seated position on the ground, and tall mint green plants towered above my head, looking gargantuan. They were pokey when I reached out to touch them. Dark triangles echoed the shapes of slender pine trees in a lake, each one having a double opposite it. One pointing up, the other pointing down, I pictured lines coming out of each, all circling through me and back to nature once again. I was connected; an integral part of the living world around me.

The drive had a turnoff for a viewpoint with access to a trail called Jenny Lake Loop. Getting there had been such a major feat, I simply wanted to lay down in the sunshine. I walked down the path and found a big rock to lay on to look at my mountains, The Tetons. The view was of a section known as the Cathedral Group, the tallest peaks in the park, and my energy climbed up just as high.

The wind picked up as a storm front blew in and my shawl and things began whirling around me. The singing birds went mute as the trees began to bend and sway. Upon feeling the first drop I made my way back to the car. A steady rain began to fall on my windshield as I said goodbye to my mountains, as if the world were crying at our parting.

At a sign for Chapel of the Sacred Heart up the road, I turned in, intrigued by its name. It was a log cabin with an interior entirely constructed of dark wood. There were only a few windows so it remained dim even in the daytime. The feature of interest was a circular stained glass window at the front of the chapel. At its center was a sacred heart; a crown of thorns sitting atop the ruby red shape with flames bursting out. It felt like I walked into my own sacred heart upon entering that building. I had neglected so much of myself in previous years, cobwebs forming in the corners of forgotten rafters and dust collecting in the darkened nooks and crannies. I was ready to let color and light back in as I communed with my higher self in the stillness.

The sun streamed in through the stained glass window, painting my once grey dress green, purple, orange, and yellow. Tiny specks of dust swirled through the air having been upset by my interruption, scattering like confetti as they looked for a new place to land. I took in a few deep breaths of the stale timber air and got up to exit, turning once when opening the door to look back at the current state of my heart, viewing it with acceptance.

As Maude crossed a bridge over Jackson Lake Dam, I looked to my left and about wrecked her into the cement barrier on the side of the road.

"*W-O-W!*" I announced.

After turning around, I drove back, parked, and crossed the street to stare at the most magnificent view I had ever laid eyes on. The Tetons catapulted toward the cosmos out of the peaceful nothingness of Jackson Lake! I began to crack up laughing, the sight was so unbelievable! The rains from earlier in the day had lifted and I ran down to the water, quickly taking off my outer layer of clothing down to my swimsuit to lay back and sunbathe as the sapphire lake splashed cold on my legs.

The roar of the water rushing through the dam rolled around in my head like thunder. It combined with the constant flow of cars that sounded like ocean waves crashing onto the shore as they passed on the road behind me. My soul was as white and bright as a thousand suns! As I laid there I shouted affirmations in my head:

> "*Thank you, Universe!*
>
> *Thank you, God!*
>
> *Thank you, me!*
>
> *I'm a lot stronger than I thought!*
>
> *I forgive myself!*
>
> *I love myself!*
>
> *I am awake!*
>
> *I am alive!*
>
> *I'm a brand new creature!*"

I couldn't believe that day, or the adventure I had been on, was my life. Everyday I saw and experienced the most thrilling things because every day I was someplace new. My losses had been so destructive it was like the world wasn't big enough for me. I just kept running, leaving one more piece of my brokenness behind with each turn of Maude's tires.

I had lived through my first non-wedding anniversary after our divorce and the one year anniversary of the day I finalized it, even recreating the day complete with veggie burger, fries, and strawberry shake. I knew in years to follow they would become just another day, hopefully ones I'd forget altogether, but because they were the first, they felt like something to celebrate.

After ten years of marriage, year eleven also marked year one. It wasn't until those anniversaries rolled around that the full weight of the loss hit me for the first time. I shoved down most of my feelings about the end of my marriage when my dad died. I had to put out the biggest fire first, and that one took over. When I awoke to the dawning of my secondary grief, the undertow about took me with it. *Oh yeah, I'm divorced... that hurts, too.* There was no way of fully knowing the extent of what I was stepping into when I walked out our front door.

All of my stories past and present were now singular; I, me, and my. No longer us, we, or ours. Even if we did them together, the shift to the singular was made, because I was just that: single. I didn't want to explain to one more person that I *was* married. We were separated for good, for keeps, forever.

"Not only do we lose our spouse through divorce, we lose our memories," a friend told me, who had also suffered through a painful separation.

There comes a solid point in recovery after a divorce or loss of any major relationship when no one wants to hear about old what's his name (or her name) anymore. But how is one supposed to forget and never again talk about such a giant part of their life? Even when I no longer wanted to bring him up, sometimes it just happened. A simple introduction had the ability to throw me off.

"How did ya'll meet?" asks someone of a friend and I.

"Through my ex," I say before thinking because that's the answer.

"What was his name?" they ask... and all of a sudden his face is the only thing in my brain.

It was like a rug I kept tripping over, *But this isn't how things were supposed to be!* I was ready to get rid of that rug. In an attempt to resolve my feelings I had even revisited where we got married months before.

"Don't go burning the place to the ground! Are you feeling stable!?" a friend had probed that morning.

Although my visit appeared to be a stroke of insanity, the tone of my visit was one of curiosity. Did that place hold some mystical key to unlock my freedom from him? Since we tied the knot there, could I now untie it there, too?

Once I made the turn down that country lane towards an old bed and breakfast in Virginia, I couldn't believe what I was doing. I was driving to the place where my marriage began; where we had our rehearsal dinner, exchanged vows and rings, and had our first dance as husband and wife. It took every ounce of bravery I had to go back.

When I pulled into the long driveway I slowed to a crawl. The once manicured lawn and shrubbery were now overgrown. Just as lovely. They were wild and free like me. I had the place to myself aside from a few sweet pups that followed everywhere I went. My companions' wagging tales and cold-nosed nudges brightened the day.

Frosty dew on the grass melded together with the warmth of the rising sun causing a giant cloud to escape from the ground. Like the earth was smoldering, recovering from a burn. I sat down and skimmed my hands over the wet blades of grass and closed my eyes to feel the place, sending myself back in time. Who was I that day eleven years before? What was I thinking? How was I feeling?

I took in each layer of that young girl. I loved her exactly as she was, unconditionally, and thanked her for each flaw, idiosyncrasy, and even her naive ideals; they made her real. I came to pay homage to her spirit, desires, and dreams. A flood swept me up as I surfed the wave that was, grateful for all that I experienced that day and since. We were lucky to have a love like that in our lifetime. I meant every word of my vows that I promised on our wedding day and intended on keeping them until the day that I die.

A part of me felt like a failure, a disappointment to myself, to my once partner, and even to God. I thought he was *the one*. The only one then, now, and forever. I began to cry as I apologized to my past self, since things didn't work out like she planned.

"I'm sorry your heart was broken. You didn't deserve that. You are worthy! You are enough! I love you, and always will," I said aloud as I covered my hands over my chest.

I could envision my dad walking me down the aisle. At the end of it he placed my hand in my beloved's. How was it possible that both of the men from that memory had evaporated from my life? I wept realizing I was the only one left standing there; the man who gave me away and the man he gave me to were both gone. Now my hands were empty, with no one to hold them. The vision fresh in my mind became the steam rising from the ground; up in smoke.

I had a sudden thought and ran down the patch of grass where the aisle had been to where we stood that day with our hands clasped together and envisioned taking my hand from his. Then I pivoted and ran back down it, away from him, breaking our bond. I was there to hold my own hand.

"I'm free! This is what freedom feels like!" I sang out. Crashing into the overgrown lawn, I bowed to my former self. "Thank you! I'm releasing you today! You are free to fly and find a new way in the world!"

A cycle of forgiveness and release moved through me as I began to finally let him, and all I thought we'd be, go. I loved myself that much. I was ready to be alone, truly radiant, truly free.

His love for me had changed, expired from what it once was, as it had with every romantic relationship I'd been in since. For the majority of my adventure, I was on my own. That was all too clear when I looked around the empty interior of my car. There were a few men I cared for at different points that I would see once in a great while, all of them longtime trusted friends, but these attempts were messy as I hadn't dated since I was a teenager. Now in my mid-thirties, I was just as clumsy as back then.

During a really dark time in my life, they brought light, fun, and reintroduced me to fragments of myself that were long forgotten; my love of painting, the thrill of seeing music preformed live, and my desire to travel. They kept me company at a distance while I was on the road, becoming a voice of confidence for me when I had little to none. Each ignited passions in me that had been dormant for a long time as they helped piece my heart back together. It was a chance to explore past my traumas to discover what I need and want in a partner.

To be clear, not all of my dating experiences were rosy and wonderful. There were a lot of lonely nights, ghosting (which I hadn't been aware was a thing—an unfriendly way of dropping someone), and my heart was constantly in a back and forth of needing someone and wanting to be alone. I skipped dating apps since meeting someone totally new scared me to death. The hardest experience I had to endure was going through a miscarriage alone, a sadness that may well last a lifetime.

In my overall collective experience, truly loving led to losing and I didn't want to go through that again. I became frightened by love, intimacy, and even happiness since I had come to equate those words with heartbreak. I didn't know if it would ever be possible for me to be with someone in a fully honest and vulnerable way again. It became my pattern to turn down opportunities for love, too scared to even try, whether it was an old boyfriend from high school or a new man I just met. When they asked me out I completely closed off and had no idea what to do, shutting them down before even giving it a chance. It seemed easier than fumbling love and getting hurt again.

Each of my attempts post divorce could have compounded my cynicism, nothing in this world lasts, but there was no room in my heart to harbor any resentments or regret. That would end up injuring me far worse than it ever could anyone else. I wasn't willing to give bitterness that power over my life.

Even though I knew he would always love me, my dad's love transformed when he died. It morphed from the physical to the ethereal. I was assured continually that I had the unfailing love of my family and friends with me always, but at the end of the day, I only had myself. I knew what it meant to love and be loyal to another person. That year I learned to love and be loyal to myself.

I got up, standing strong and tall in mountain pose, looking at my mountains, The Tetons. With my shoulders relaxed, arms at my sides, and serene expression; my posture was one of complete surrender. I envisioned solid impenetrable roots growing down through my body. Grounded and connected with the earth, I became the mountains I was admiring.

Then I made a new vow: to be confident in myself and my choices. Whether I was destined to have a series of loves during different seasons, the forever love I always dreamed of finding, or continued down the path of self-love I'd been on, my heart would be open. I would always be a bit of a hopeless romantic, but I could trust my intuition. No matter where I might find myself, I could always find a sense of belonging, wholeness, and home within me. I didn't need to be scared of losing someone else, because I would never lose myself again.

it's an adventure

A friend I grew up with was back in our hometown visiting from her new home in California. After spending the day together she held me by the shoulders and looked straight at me, her lips curled in a smile.

"Do you want to drive out to the west coast together?" she asked.

She had planned to fly back, but knew in recent days I was down for a good road trip. I was planning to drive to Oregon for a flight out of Portland to the final state of my solo adventure. It was the only one I couldn't get to by car; Hawaii. Some flight attendant friends were helping me with affordable tickets there and back. It would mean a large southern detour, but nothing was holding me back.

"Sure, let's do it!" I told her.

We spent the night at her parents' house before we left and I enjoyed the guest room to myself as we prepared for our long journey. There was something comfortable and familiar about that place. The family photos that lined the stairwell, the way her mom practiced songs for church on the piano while the news ran on the TV in the next room, the smell of her dad's paintings in his art studio downstairs, and their pool we used to play in as kids that I had a midnight yoga session beside that night.

Since my things didn't take up much room, we went about packing the last of her belongings that were in storage at her parents' house into the car. Maude was stuffed to the gills. Although saying goodbye to her mom in the driveway felt different for my friend, it was like I was saying goodbye to my own childhood, my own mother, my own house, too.

"Love you!" we both hollered out our open windows as we backed out of their driveway into the suburban street. I put us in drive and we were gone.

On our cross-country road trip beginning in Illinois, we made stops in Missouri, Oklahoma, Texas, Arizona, California, and Nevada. We reconnected with old friends, volunteered with disaster relief for a hurricane that had hit Houston, met two of my closest friends' baby in the hospital a few days after she was born, hiked a mountain in the desert at night, and ran along the beach through the waves of the Pacific Ocean together. A lifetime of experiences in just a few short weeks. For the last part of our trip we even picked up a mascot, her cat. Imagine two women trying to sleep in a car at a truck stop in Las Vegas with a cat wandering around.

"Is this really our life!?" we laughed.

One afternoon I glanced over to see her crying in the passenger seat. She was heartsick over a devastating breakup. It's what I must have looked like the entire time I was driving alone. The highway ahead of us was reflected in the tears sitting just below her eyes, whole galaxies shimmering in each drop.

Although we knew how to have fun and had plenty of it on our trip, we challenged one another, were introduced to new ideas, and even argued a few times. Our personalities and friendship are like the perfect yin and yang, each of us assuming different roles in different moments. We were both on the verge of something new and held each other's hand as we drove through the transition.

Once we parted I made my way to the last of my landmark destinations, my wonders of America, Big Sur, California. I had dreamed of seeing that coastline for months and sang to myself as I flew from the car. My excitement catapulted me out of the vehicle! The wind off the cliffs caught me, held me, and took my breath away. Then the view did it for a second time. I became something new. Always do. Every time. It affects me internally, my chemical makeup shifts, and my superpowers are restored; the ocean brings me back to life.

"*I did it!*" I cried. Somehow I made it everywhere I had hoped to go, a bittersweet triumph. Joy overcame me, having made it to them all, but there was also a lingering visceral sadness; perhaps I was looking at the end of the journey.

That night I pulled into a rest area outside of San Francisco hoping to find a place to sleep. I got one of the last parking spots around 7 PM as the sun was starting to set and send the sky into fits of scarlet and cadmium orange. The parking lot became a horizontal hotel for sleepy sojourners. Some drivers danced around their cars preparing their makeshift bedrooms before dark. They shoved blankets, towels, and sweaters into their slightly lowered windows to keep out the blinding security lights of the parking lot; curtains for their mini rooms that night. Then, just as surely as every night, the sky turned black. The lot fell eerily quiet and the blinds on the world slowly shut as I closed my eyes.

I made numerous stops at resale stores and pawn shops up the coast, anything to help fuel the last leg of my adventure. I'd look through the contents of my car and ask myself, "What can I part with?" then put together a bag of non-essentials and stroll into stores with hopes they'd want something. At this point it wasn't uncommon to open my trunk as employees looked over my shoulder.

"You want any of this stuff?" I'd ask.

That trip I sold my winter coat, most of my clothing, sneakers, an external hard drive, pocket knives, my tripod, and even those "dancing lady in the desert" earrings from my first big trip to Utah. I had become the dancing lady in the desert and had to part with them to continue to be so. The things I could bare to pawn, trade, or sell were dwindling. Almost all of my belongings were now gone from my trunk. I was nearly out of resources.

It wasn't until I was sitting outside the airport in Maui that my body began to shut down. It had all been building to that moment. My trip had come to it's completion. Taking my sandals off and putting my toes into that carpet of deep green grass, it felt so final.

I hadn't seen the friend I stayed with in more than ten years, having shared the classrooms of some of our first photography classes together. In the time we were apart we uncannily shared similar life experiences, and just like so many years before, I felt a deep connection with her. I spent most of my days in the cradle of a hammock in her backyard. It held me as I studied the broad avocado tree that shaded me, listened to it's rustling leaves, and let it comfort me. I was recovering. High healing warm vibrations went through each pore of my skin and out again, circulating energy in and through me.

As I walked along the beach one day I let my feet sink deeper into the sand of the final state on my journey. The staggering achievement I made filled me up! Over the course of a year and a half, I saw all fifty states in the United States of America! Many of them multiple times.

It wasn't my initial goal to see all of them. I had been to the Big Island with my family as a child, but with the added expense and factors of flying, Hawaii had not made the cut during my solo road trip. Once

I made it to forty-nine states on my own, my friend's daughters urged me to see all fifty. With three girls under the age of eleven, their house in Cincinnati was one giant sleepover every night of the week. I not only got to reconnect with my friend and her husband, whom I first met in the dorms in college, I became friends with their children.

"You're so close! You only have one left!" the three of them shrilled. I promised them I'd try.

Whether to see friends, national parks, or just because, with well over 150,000 miles under my belt, I made it to all of them. That milage is about six trips around the earth! Looking at all fifty written together I feel the victory: Alabama, Alaska, Arizona, Arkansas, California, Colorado, Connecticut, Delaware, Florida, Georgia, Hawaii, Idaho, Illinois, Indiana, Iowa, Kansas, Kentucky, Louisiana, Maine, Maryland, Massachusetts, Michigan, Minnesota, Mississippi, Missouri, Montana, Nebraska, Nevada, New Hampshire, New Jersey, New Mexico, New York, North Carolina, North Dakota, Ohio, Oklahoma, Oregon, Pennsylvania, Rhode Island, South Carolina, South Dakota, Tennessee, Texas, Utah, Vermont, Virginia, Washington, West Virginia, Wisconsin, and Wyoming!

It really is America the beautiful; stunning, inspirational, spiritual beauty. Her miles upon miles of rolling fields, overwhelming mountain ranges, endless forests to explore, and mysterious rivers lifted my weary grief-stricken heart. My drive had been a procession through my homeland, with banners held high in memory of my father and past life. I stayed down and broken for a long while, incapable of finding the healing I so craved as I made my way down each exit ramp off the highway. The hours upon hours on the open road provided time and privacy to talk things out, cry, scream, shout, dance, and sing; the sounds only rattling through that five by nine foot space. Mile after lonely mile, I was finding myself out there on the freeways of America. That's just it, I was going a *free way*.

When I first set out I began collecting small items at each stop; a feather I found in Little Rock, Arkansas, a shell while walking the beach with a friend in Massachusetts, and a small piece of metal on the sidewalk in Philadelphia. I placed them all in the middle console of my car. It was a way to take each place with me. I've since put many of them into a dreamcatcher I made to remind me of my trip across the country. With each new place I picked up a new part of myself.

In Big Sur earlier that week, I gazed at the ocean and sent love to all the people and parts of the world that were unknown to me. Looking across the endless ocean from Hawaii towards the distant shores of home, I felt my own blessing as it washed over me. After holding it for a moment I sent that same loving-kindness back to everyone I knew and to the life I'd be returning to.

While on the island, one of my flight attendant friends who helped get me there flew in with work. It was actually one of the women I met at Liard River Hot Springs in Canada! She knew what my journey meant to me and made it possible to complete it. We had a few hours to share together and spent them celebrating and lounging by the pool at her hotel. Laying next to her, soaking in the sun in another part of the world, I felt our souls aligning like planets eclipsing each other, a union like none other.

My last night in Hawaii the friend I stayed with made us a feast fit for the queens that we are. As her puppy sat curled at our feet, and our bellies were full, she placed one of her dog's toys on the table and instructed me to put who I was at the beginning of my trip into the doll.

"It's time to honor yourself and all you've been through. You don't need that small, scared, weak girl anymore," she told me. "You've outgrown her! Tell her that! Tell her that you're leaving her behind. *Scream it if you have to!*"

I could feel the doubtful little girl in me fall away like an old skin. I *had* outgrown her! *"I'm leaving you here!"* I yelled. *"Goodbye old life!"*

Once back on the mainland I began making the pilgrimage to Illinois once again for the one year anniversary of Poppy's passing, which didn't seem real somehow. The moon was almost full and hanging low, lighting everything to the farthest my vision could take me. And I began to think of him, as I do every time I see the moon. The ground appeared to fall away from the sky. The earth became a black paper cutout, silhouetted by a deep grey plane above, speckled in sparkling pinholes. New constellations formed in every space around as my headlights hit the reflectors on guardrails and the double lines down the center of the road. Both dippers hung magically in midair above them, pouring power over my trip, the last one of my tour.

Hills along the roadside were like waves in the ocean, layered in a white foamy fog. Light and shadows danced between the street lights and my skin casting a warm glow in never-ending looping patterns; one after another after another. I slowed when approaching a thick fog, then submerged like a submarine, and after a few breaths was up in the open air again.

The long slow lull of the drive brought me into a calm state the next few days. I drove southeast through Wyoming, and as the sun began to rise, noticed the layers of color etched through the earth across the Great Plains. A purple layer, deep ochre, and brown; a vibrant earth tapestry. A long black tanker train and a yellow airplane flying over a nearby field spraying it with a white cloud were the only company with the same early bird schedule as me. As I entered Nebraska, rain streaked down in long teal swoops over jade hills, freckling the windows, making the universe and all in it quiet.

As the light in the sky began to fade to end another day, a truck in front of me went over the ridge of the earth like a sinking ship, bobbing up and down with the waves of the pavement. His lights came up again and then sank beneath the surface of the horizon, disappearing into the darkness. A trail of headlights came toward me steadily, in small increments of one or two cars at a time.

Eventually it was all trucks in both directions, and soon they also bedded down for the night. I was the only passenger car at 4:30 in the morning. Tractor trailers were like big fish sleeping in the ocean deep as they filled exit and entrance ramps bumper to bumper in the wee hours of the morning. Large shadows that appeared suddenly against the faint light of the night sky. With their lights off and drivers sleeping in their cabs, I quietly tiptoed by them as I rolled down the expressway; my radio singing them a lullaby low and soft. I felt like a mama hen trying not to disturb her baby chicks. I wanted a little more time by myself out there on the road.

Sailing through Iowa and into Missouri southbound on Interstate 29, it was a calm straight sea with slight ups and downs as we continued to sink down in sea level. I had never been on that highway before and liked the ebb and flow of it. I'm sure the truckers enjoyed taking the road in that direction; a slight downgrade with little effort involved or necessary.

The listlessness of the drive had me reflecting on the lengths my trip had taken me, having connected the dots of many places in dad's life after he was gone. My aunt helped me locate their father, mother, and brother's gravesites across the country and each of the homes they grew up in. When I pulled into the driveway of the house they remembered best, I pictured my dad and his sister running through the yard as kids laughing and playing. The land sloped around it hugging the home, a stretch of woods lined the yard in back, and birds sang to me from the nature all around. It was reminiscent of my parents' house, almost like he rebuilt the memory. As I turned around in front of the garage to leave, I imagined my dad going through the front door as a child, waving at me with a smile from behind the pane of glass.

I also visited places in my own history. My sister and I went back to the house we grew up in and the owner gave us a welcoming look around. We could see every stage of ourselves as soon as we walked through the front door. There we were putting on shows with our friends in our leotards and tutu's in the living room, smelling mom's homemade meals as we walked into the kitchen, then up the stairs to our playroom where we dressed our dog up in costumes and had tea parties with our dolls, the pretty blue and white floral wallpaper I picked out still adorning the walls of the bedroom that had been mine once I was old enough for my own room, and out back to the garden where we planted vegetables with dad.

I visited every place my ex and I lived as well; there were nine in our ten years together, which spanned five states. I also went by where I lived during college and a few apartments I had during that time, which added two more states to the list. Each place chipped away something I had been hiding under. Having no address when visiting them, they helped me form a vision of where I hoped to go.

As I came through the door of my parents' house for my final homecoming, our year of firsts would be complete as of midnight that night. The first birthdays, Thanksgiving, my parents' wedding anniversary, Christmas, New Years, Father's Day, the day of his passing, and all the other days of the year. No calls, outings, talks, or hugs... we made it the first full year without him.

As was the case with most big days, none of us could remember what we did for Christmas the year before, confirming we were all out of it at the time. No one felt much like celebrating a family holiday without the whole family. We didn't put up the tree or decorate the yard the first year, since Dad always had the lead on that. Even sitting at the dining room table without his presence at the head of it was unbearable, surely to send one, if not all of us, into sobs. I bought a miniature tree about as tall as my niece and nephew last minute so they could open presents under it. There would have been nothing had it not been for them. Their little hearts kept us all going.

The second Christmas after he died would be decidedly different. Our family had its first real Christmas without Poppy, and the last one in his house. Mom would be moving into a smaller home the following month. In light of this, she decided to have our last traditional family gathering at the house, use her china and the whole nine. As we held hands and sang our family prayer we've sung since my sister and I were young, I looked at the head of the table where Dad always sat. Empty now, a few battery-powered candles sitting at his place on the table; a safer way of remembering with two toddlers in the house.

We ate off our parents' wedding china for the first time since he passed away and sat at the table long after we were done eating, talking like we always used to. The kids enjoyed playing with their new three-wheeled scooters from Santa while we did so. We were remembering how to celebrate again, how to laugh again. Yes, we talked about him a lot that day, cried a bit even, and that was a good thing.

The house was different, our parents' belongings were clearing out slowly as Mom downscaled for her new home. It was too hard for her to live there anymore. What began as a new start for the two of them, having finished building that house after my sister and I left the nest, turned into a place of grieving and longing. After bearing witness to years of illness, treatments, and finally his death, she needed another new start.

She hired an auction company a few months before to pick up many of the big furniture pieces. The idea began with her bedroom set that she and Dad picked out together when they built the house, their dream home. She couldn't live with the constant reminder that her bed and subsequent life were now half empty.

"Are you sure you want to do this?" I asked her before they came to take it away.

"That bed is just too big for one person," she told my sister and I. "And every time I roll over and see the empty spot where your dad used to be I go through losing him all over again. I slept in a twin bed before I married your father. Why wouldn't I go back to one now that he's gone?" After forty years of being with someone, I don't know how one could feel any other way.

We played tag in the empty basement, took our first family photo minus one in front of the fireplace on a timer, and ended the day with a dance party. As my sister and her husband got ready to leave to get the kids in bed at home, we shared one of our famous group hugs. Someone hollers, "Family hug!" and everyone comes running. It's the best when my niece calls for it with, "Bamawe Hug!"

"This is just how Poppy would have wanted it. Today was a great day," my brother-in-law said as we all hugged each other close.

"If you're half of him, and I'm half of him, it's kind of like we *are* him when we're together!", my sister and I discovered as the two of us embraced. When our powers combined, he showed up. Then they were off.

As Mom and I began to clear the table putting dishes in the sink, I decided to continue our dance party. I turned the volume up as *Two Can Have A Party* by Marvin Gaye and Tammi Terrell began to play, went in the kitchen, and held my hand out to her. She washed off her hands and grabbed mine as I sang to her, joining our duet as she began to cry.

"I'm so sorry, honey," she said tearfully.

"It's alright Mama, we have each other," I said. Laughing through our tears we danced and twirled one another until the song ended; just me and Mom.

A few days later one of her friends came over to help pack fragile items in preparation for her move. The boxes they packed weren't the first. Many of the closets were already stuffed with things Mom had packed over the months. As they left for the afternoon I went to look at their work. There were three large moving boxes lined up against the kitchen counter where barstools used to sit. I was surprised by the feeling that came over me. Not optimism or anticipation of the future, I felt trapped and claustrophobic.

Maude and I went out for a spin and change of scenery. I needed space and the best spot for that during winter was down at the boat slip. That time of year the Mississippi River has ice chunks broken and emerging toward the sky in hundreds of sharp points. Its entire frozen surface looked like a massive piece of crystal quartz.

Various stones always traveled with me. They promoted openness, cleansed my aura, helped bring my chakras into alignment, provided protection, and energized my capacity for love of others and of self. As I imagined the river was a gigantic gemstone, I could feel it's healing properties radiate through me.

The river was the best place to recenter myself. Each time I returned from traveling, I stopped at a parking lot across the river from where I grew up. I'd sit there for an hour or two, hypnotized by the water, adjusting to the fact that I was back again.

From where I sat I could see the back of the house I grew up in, the building dad's office was in over the bridge, and straight ahead up the river and out of sight was the town my parents lived in for the last twelve years. It was the same parking lot where dad taught my sister and I how to drive. He set up cones for us to weave through and made up parking challenges. Eventually my sister and I discovered we both went there to sit when we were missing him.

A group of migrating birds flew over me as I sat there one day. Their flight patterns collectively shifted like a swarm of bees. They soared in a curling twisting corkscrew pattern, like a school of fish in an endless ocean. They instinctually sensed one another so they could move as one and seemed to know exactly where they were going. Thousands of them went on and on without an end in sight! My mind began to open to the change that's all around us every day. It can be a really wonderful thing.

When I got back to the house I looked at those boxes again. Three: my mom, sister, and me. It was hard for all of us to see everything in that house go away. It was our most direct link to dad. We could still see him tinkering at his tool bench in the garage, falling asleep in his red rocker watching the birds at the feeder on the back porch, and standing at the kitchen counter clinking his bowl with his spoon as he ate his nighttime yogurt or ice cream. Mail was still delivered to the house for him, and if the postal service still recognized him as living, couldn't he be? I could swing by the door to his office downstairs and ask my usual, "How's it going, Dad?" and see him there looking at me clear as day. It was where he was supposed to be. He still felt alive there.

But Mom's move was happening whether we felt ready or not. By the end of the week the house would be empty and she would be moving into a new home. My sister and I walked around the house as movers began to wrap each piece of furniture with a large roll of plastic wrap. All of the memories in that place, those we could carry with us.

I stayed there a bit longer after she moved. What began as a couple of weeks turned into months. Even though I was isolated in that big empty house all by myself, I was used to that way of living from my time on the road. My minimalist belongings became its only contents. The majority of my things fit neatly in front of the fireplace: sleeping bag, some blankets, a pillow, and bag of clothes. A few items went in a kitchen drawer and toiletries were in one of the bathrooms. It felt like a massive tent I was squatting in.

Change is hard for me. It's like my day at Horseshoe Bend in Arizona. I dug my heels into the earth. I was terrified of that ledge. There I was, faced with a metaphorical ledge on the precipice of something new. *"But I'm not ready! I'm scared!"* screamed everything inside of me.

There was such a push and pull every time I left home; the comforts, the people, and the way things used to be. In the back of my mind I knew my departure was only temporary. I'd be back to my hometown for the next holiday, birthday in the family, or for a friend's event planned the next month. Maude and I created a continual infinity loop as we crossed the country and back again. In all of my time away, no matter how far my wanderlust took me, I could always come back to my parents' house and gather the horses again. What would life be like without that constant to depend on? While Mom wanted us to think of her new house the same way, how could it be home if Dad had never been there?

I knew it was a good step for us to leave, it would be best for all of us moving forward, but I hated that it was. My sadness was like a heavy down comforter I wrapped myself up in. Once I left that place I knew I'd miss the weight of it. During that time someone told me, "His house holds the last portrait of him in your mind," and I wanted to protect that picture. I didn't want to lose it.

Maude still hummed along even after the beating our drive had put her through. She gave me the occasional escape when I needed to leave the house. One evening on a backroad through the country, her engine suddenly gave out. I coasted up to the top of the hill I was on, rocking back and forth trying to add to her momentum. I pulled into the entrance of someone's driveway and pleaded with her, *"Please, please, please!"* and she restarted. I took her to a shop the following day and awaited the news of what the damage would be. The call I received later that week was not what I expected.

"I'm sorry, but your car needs a new engine," I was told. "It cracked right down the middle and isn't drivable in this condition." It would have cost the same as buying a new car to replace it, so I made one of the hardest decisions I've ever had to make, and let her go, too. In the process of healing my heart, at 250,000 miles, hers finally gave out.

Maude represented freedom. She gave me wings to escape my marriage, run away once my dad died, and helped me find my own new path. She got me all the way to Alaska and back, the farthest north I had ever been. The three cracks in her windshield were my trophies from the drive through Canada, the first time I was out of the country by myself. She also crossed the Seven Mile Bridge to Key West at the southernmost tip of Florida, the farthest south I had ever driven.

Like a friend or family member you travel with, I have photos and selfies with my constant companion. "Here's Maude on our way to Red Rock Canyon in Nevada!", or "Last night we camped at the foothills of the Guadalupe Mountains in Texas!" and "Look, she made it all the way up to Niagara Falls in New York!" She became my friend through both the darkest and brightest season I've ever known.

The day I collected my belongings from her, I had to let go of the last physical piece that connected me to my dad, who gave her to me, the loss of my marriage, and my past self. Together we saw forty-nine states. She made my trip possible. She also made a large portion of this book possible. With the insurance money and various sums I received when she died, I was able to pay to develop the film from my trip. She helped me finish this whole thing.

After seeing so much and traveling so far, it was finally time to be still. I knew my days at Poppy's house wouldn't last forever, so I cherished each one. I made bonfires with wood from Dad's woodpile, logs he cut with an axe and his own two hands. I visited the tree and bench that the neighbors placed in memory of him at the park up the street, went for walks in the woods to talk to the deer and birds he used to care for, and ran circuits in the graveyard at the edge of the neighborhood. I had conversations with each of the departed, weeded around their headstones, and picked up decorations that had blown across the lawn, often feeling like those laid to rest were the only ones who could truly understand me.

To wake each day I began with meditation, sun salutations, and spiritual readings in the front bedroom. It was empty aside from curtains, so I could choose any spot to begin my practice. My usual choice was where Dad's armchair used to be. He'd sit there, speckled in morning light while he read his Bible and daily devotion. It was his favorite room in the house. The whites and teals mom decorated it in reminded him of the beach. The sunrise shone brightly on my face through the bay window, which I always left open (the same one open the night he died). A bright red cardinal that roosted on the front entry light often came to visit me on a tree branch outside of it.

"Hi Dad," I'd say to him. The little bird would tilt his head looking at me quizzically. It was the room he left us in. In a wonderful way it became my sanctuary, my place to find him.

Thanks to the recommendation of a friend that lived across the street, I got my first job waiting tables, even though I had zero experience, at one of the only places in walking distance downtown. The new friends I worked with and served welcomed me back to the land of the living and brought a lightness and humor into every day. There were birthday parties, kids hula hooping and drawing with colorful sidewalk chalk, cover bands that played late into the evening on weekends, and smiles all around. Having been the last place we went as a family before dad passed away, occasionally after a long shift, I'd go sit near the river where we sat that day and talk with him like I did on the road.

I tucked away my earnings and each lucky penny I found while sweeping the floor of the restaurant, "pennies from heaven" as Mom would say. I was saving up for my next big adventure: my first solo backpacking trip through Europe, a dream I never thought possible to do by myself before surmounting my tour of America.

The youngest and last of my bridesmaids to wed was getting married in Scotland. My wedding had come full circle. I was the first of my friends to marry, and soon would be the only one single again. They have always been treasured jewels in my life. I've known all six of them since before we hit double-digits in age and we're still as close as sisters. They were not only there for the beginning of life with my ex, they formed the foundation of support I needed when I left. I decided if I was flying all the way there I wouldn't be turning around after one week. Since driving was no longer possible when traveling, I'd look into other modes, and training between countries became the next one. At the end of the summer, I would spend three months abroad.

Since the house was empty and I lived by myself, I could set up my yoga mat anywhere, have dance parties at all hours of the day or night, and my voice echoed like I was in a concert hall as I sang as loud as I wanted. The open spaces and hardwood floors allowed my body and spirit to frolic around positively carefree. It was a time of grounding, seeking balance, and finding harmony within.

Throughout my journey I sought out various healing avenues spanning conventional therapy, medical specialists, various energy healers and intuitives, tarot readings, tapping, gong baths, and an assortment of other experiences. I added to this list while staying at Poppy's house with regular massages, acupuncture sessions, and chiropractic adjustments; each a conscious step towards repairing my mind, body, and soul. Having been on the road so long without consistent care, my physical body was falling apart. I also communicated with friends online, traveling to distant lands all from my house in the woods.

Diving into self-discovery, I experimented with the most perplexing items at the supermarket in the one pot I purchased. I tried ingredients I had never used before like dragonfruit, endive, cherimoya, kohlrabi, horned melon, turmeric root, and couscous. I'd layer the bottom of my shopping basket with one of each new-to-me item (they always loved me in the checkout line). I was finding my own preferences and what I liked when there was no one to decide what to buy but me, eventually deciding on a primarily vegan lifestyle.

The sum of my belongings mirrored the day I left my ex three years before; a small bag with clothing, toiletries, my laptop, and a few books. I hadn't put down roots since I left him, and was scared to commit to a new city, apartment, job, or relationship. What if that blew up too? During my days of solace, I began to look forward to all of the new adventures life could still hold. Maybe there could be love after divorce. Maybe there could be life after death. Little by little, I was crawling my way back.

After my last day as a waitress, I threw away my uniform, tennis shoes, and apron. Packing my one box of belongings into the back of mom's car, I was ready to shove off into the future. In three years time, I would explore all fifty states in the United States of America, many of our national parks, and twenty-one other countries, an odyssey I had no foreknowledge of the day I left my old life.

I made it to many countries that were lifelong hopefuls (plus some) including Austria, Belgium, Canada, Czech Republic, Denmark, Finland, France, Germany, Iceland, Ireland, Italy, Luxembourg, Mexico, Netherlands, Norway, Poland, Portugal, Spain, Sweden, Switzerland, and The United Kingdom (Scotland, England, and Wales).

While backpacking through Europe I'd experience art I had always dreamed of seeing, learn to speak through charades when there was a language barrier (which threw my fear and pride out the window), and found that loss transcends borders. I saw an exhibition about poppies in Wales where I learned it's a flower of remembrance in many parts of the world, went on a hike to see a spectacular view of the fjords from an overlook in Norway with a new friend named Jorge (one of my guideposts in another language), and cried with a man on a night train through Poland as he tried to tell me about his brother's sudden passing in broken English. Just like in America, there were divine circumstances and people at every turn to reaffirm that I was not alone.

I would also decide to take back my maiden name after some friends in Switzerland translated it; a German word that means, "heroes." As I trained between countries and walked through foreign cities with only my backpack as company, I was reinventing myself. Just like my dream in the desert, I was becoming someone new. I was becoming my own hero. Upon returning to the states it would be my first line of business—reclaim my name.

The most life-changing part of this trip was discovering my own spirituality through ancient sites and services in every tradition and tongue. I followed the footsteps of Mary Magdeline in the South of France on a sacred feminine pilgrimage with a friend who had also gone through a divorce and her own father's passing in our years apart, took my first communion since I was young in Portugal (finally feeling welcome at the table), and rededicated my life to Spirit in Sweden at a service in large part I didn't understand. Even though unfamiliar languages were being spoken in these places, God got through.

While not holding to all of the same beliefs as my parents, ancestors, or what I was taught as a child, I found a spirituality and understanding of my own. One that changes in form, expands with my experiences, and grows each day. History came alive in those places, and so did my relationship with a power higher and greater than me. My year in the glories of nature while on my tour of the United States began to chip away at my past religious hurts and disbelief. Europe helped bring that part of my journey full circle.

Whether you call it God, Spirit, Universe, Energy, or what have you, I believe as seekers, we are all on a path to find the same source. As such, I will discover pieces of that light entity my whole life through. I don't claim to have all the answers, those are slowly revealed one by one, but I will spread a message of love, forgiveness, and friendship because they've been given to me.

When I first set out on my own, a friend showed me a silver turtle figurine she was given when she was little. There was a castle built on top of its shell.

"A turtle takes her home with her," she told me.

After traveling many miles, feeling lost, placeless, and at times homeless staying in locations far and wide, I'm still unsure of where life is taking me. Although that could give rise to fear, and some days it does more than others, I choose to infuse each moment with radical joy after my year of losses, or life of gain's as a friend rephrased it. I'll keep walking, taking each day one step at a time regardless if the destination is uncertain.

"It's an adventure!" as Dad would say.

After driving by Poppy's house one evening once it sold to say my last goodbyes, I drove down the Great River Road between Grafton and Alton, Illinois along the Mississippi River on a twelve mile stretch that I like to call "Dad's road." We went on countless family bike rides on the path next to it growing up, it's where he photographed eagles later in life, and one day when we're ready, it's where he wanted his ashes to be scattered.

When I first got my driver's license at sixteen, it was my favorite road. I would drive it back and forth with nowhere to go, imagining I was on my way to somewhere else. It's not that I didn't like it there, I'm proud of where I come from, I just wanted to see what lay beyond it. During my years of travel it became my entrance to life on the road and the long driveway home when I returned. I even hoofed the entire length of it one day to work through some things, an attempt to get a fresh perspective.

As I drove, I envisioned each freeway I experienced across this great country. All of a sudden I was on a coastal highway, the mighty river changing into a crystal blue ocean stretching as far as I could see to my right. The bluffs to my left transformed into a soaring mountain ridge scraping the sky. As I weaved in and out with the bends in the road it was like I was dodging between tall redwoods somewhere deep in the forest, the wind whipping through my hair freeing my spirit once more. Barge lights looked like lighthouses with their beams sweeping across the water, searching all night long. All of the places I had been, and would one day ever see, could combine into that one road.

visual diary

Grafton, Illinois

Grafton, Illinois

Grafton, Illinois

Unknown Location

Santa Fe, New Mexico

White Sands National Park, New Mexico

Arches National Park, Utah

Capitol Reef National Park, Utah

Big Bend National Park, Texas

Crater Lake National Park, Oregon

North Cascades National Park, Washington

Olympic National Park, Washington

Near the Alaska/Canada Border

Yellowstone National Park, Wyoming

Craters of the Moon National Monument and Preserve, Idaho

Grand Teton National Park, Wyoming

Big Sur, California

Grafton, Illinois

Grafton, Illinois

Grafton, Illinois

The Great River Road near Grafton, Illinois

afterward

For some time now, I've toyed with the idea of including an update of sorts to end this beloved tale. My 50 state adventure has long-since passed, but I've found it continues, perhaps it will my whole life through. In this moment I'm cozied up in a huge king-sized bed at a hotel in northern Mississippi on my way to a healing photography retreat with a friend I mentioned previously. She is one of my Santa Fe sisters who lost her Mom in the process of writing this book. My journey has come full circle in a sense.

As I spoke with the concierge to see if there was an affordable room to stay in tonight, I noticed the lovely name on his nametag, George, and an immediate calm encompassed my entire being. As we spoke of travel, he mentioned his family lived in cities all across the United States.

"After my mom and dad died everyone kind of spread out across the country," he said.

Awakened from my tired stupor, I replied, "Did you just say both of your parents passed away?"

The answer was yes, both in the past year. While I empathized with how horrible that must have been, he told me he was grateful that he was able to take care of and be with them before it happened.

"I'm so glad I got to spend that time with them," he told me. Just as I'm glad I got to spend that time with my dad.

It wasn't until after writing the pages of *Free Way* that I realized the affect my cumulative grief had. Recently, I got remarried and many old insecurities and traumas from my past relationship resurfaced that thoroughly surprised me. I never had a doubt in my mind about my new partner, it was just fear about making a commitment and being married again. *Me? Married!? I'm not so sure about this*, went the loop of thoughts. Life can bring us many wonderful and, at times, humbling gifts if we let it. *I want to add, there are resources to support anyone in a toxic, unsafe, or abusive situation. Find help through a safe family member, friend, counselor, hospital, church, or community group if you need it. Please, don't wait.

Now almost five years after my double loss, a lot has changed by way of place and people in my life. I moved back to my hometown area of St. Louis, Missouri to be with the new man I fell in love with. He understands some of my innermost parts, also having gone through divorce and father loss in rapid succession.

In a matter of months we unfortunately went through two very painful miscarriages, the passing of his grandma, and my grandpa; knitting our hearts together even tighter. Although we have a dream of children, perhaps we are meant to come upon it in a different way than anticipated. Birthing this book into the world has been a way for me to find healing and purpose around these losses, being some of the hardest I have ever encountered.

One thing pregnancy loss brought up with a vengeance was a resurfacing of grief for my dad in a compounded, more complicated way. It was the first major thing to happen in my life since his passing and I ached to confide in him about it. He had always been the person I talked to about those things. Realizing afresh that he really isn't here, that he is gone and will be forever (at least in this lifetime) hurt so deeply. But as he told me just before he died, when I get quiet enough, I know what he'd say which is a comfort. Once again, I live near the rest of my family, and that has been a huge support during this difficult time.

During the creation stage of this book, so many people I met and know have been through a great loss. Grief is not a four letter word and can be talked about openly—it is a balm to the soul to release our stories and let the atmosphere absorb a portion of them. First, allow grief to take up some space, and it needs a lot. I've learned that time does not actually heal all wounds, or quite possibly, any of them. In my case, grief merely seeps into every part of life, not as dense or concentrated as it is at first, but still attaching to each experience, interaction, and even private moment alone.

Yet, as my new friend George in Mississippi reminded me, I would have much rather loved and been loved this fully and have the giant hole in my heart after those I love leave, than to not have it at all. Even in their passing, life is more complete and better because we've loved and been loved. It's a risk. We are going to lose the people we care about most, but it's so worth it to love big. I wouldn't have it any other way and wouldn't change a thing.

As I stopped at each truck stop, gas station, and restaurant chain the past few days, I had flashbacks to those travel days of mine. Living and learning out on the road, and I couldn't be happier to now have a home to spread my wings out in and return to, where I'm unfurling and putting my roots down deep. It can be scary not knowing where you'll lay your head at night or where your next meal is coming from.

Believe me, I had some run-ins during my journey I would have much rather skipped entirely, if I had been a little more cautious out there. At the time I was a bit careless, hardly having any regard for my life. Thank God for the bubble of protection that seemed to follow me wherever I went. I want to implore future travelers that may be inspired by my story—be careful out there my dear friends. You are so very precious, deeply loved, and this universe is richer because of your gifts and presence in it.

Lastly, I want to thank each person who supported the making of this book. It all started with a dream and my community of family and friends have helped bring it to life. Together you raised over $13,000 for the printing of these very pages, for an audiobook, ebook, and perhaps a print-to-order version online! The overflowing abundance of your generosity has absolutely amazed me. I am eternally grateful for you and your contribution. I want to leave a legacy of love, belonging, and compassion for those in grief, and you have helped make it possible.

Be good to those in grief in your life, especially yourself when it comes to knock on your own door. May you find joy in the journey and the freedom to let your light burn bright. You have a story to share as well.

With deep love and gratitude,
Rachel

with gratitude

To My Family,

My deepest heart thanks goes to you. Thank you for your openness and encouragement in the sharing of this story, of which a large part of is our story. You gave me space to breathe and grow while I was on the road, yet were waiting with open arms every time I returned. The world is a different place without Dad, but I see him daily in each of you. I'm grateful he lives on in this way. Renae, Lindsey, Derrick, Levi, Iris, Angela (and Olive, too), I'd like to dedicate this book as a gift to you.

Also, thank you Charles, the newest part of my family, for encouraging my early morning edits and endless hours of work to birth this project. Your support has been monumental.

Ten-four my dearest ones. I love each of you to the moon and back.

Extended Family and Friends,

You supported me when I needed you most and became some of my greatest teachers during my journey. Thank you for opening your hearts and homes to me, and for revealing your own stories of loss. You proved that there is still love in the world.

To each new face I met, you may not know the impact you had on my life. Thank you for showing up right when I needed you.

My Creative Community,

Thank you to my incredibly talented creative community for your energy, advice, and daily inspiration. This book was possible because of your combined support.

As for the creation of this book, thank you to Olivia Leigh Smith and Heather Brown for putting your hearts into the stunning layout of these pages and to Laura Grant Design for your thoughtful (and absolutely perfect) book cover design. Susan Burnstine, for your friendship and for taking great care in helping me organize my thoughts and images for this project. To each friend who was a beta reader, thank you for your feedback and support with editing, most especially Patty Mekhail, Erin Lawrence, and Colleen Kavanaugh. Mary Virginia Swanson, for asking the hard questions and providing clarity in the final stages of this work. And finally, to Kickstarter, for creating a brilliant platform to fund this project and Squarespace for bringing ease to the website creation process.

I am immensely grateful for the companies that hired me or gave me a cause to volunteer with along the way. You gave me purpose and a cause greater than myself to be a part of. Thank you Back Trap Yoga, Bostick & Sullivan, The Cathedral ATX, FotoFest, Games for Humanity, Glass Blowing Austin, The Grace Edition, Heart Scoop Studio, Live Nation, The Loading Dock, National Caregiving Conference, Oklahoma Shirt Company, ParaMounts Artifact and Exhibit Specialists, Parks Project, PhotoNOLA, The Portland Bark Bus, Samaritan's Purse, Share Pregnancy and Infant Loss Support, Siteman Cancer Center, St. Louis Cardinals, Tailgate Guys, Tri-Township Library, Yellowstone Forever, and Yoga Buzz.

To my photo community, thank you to the staff, instructors, and participants at the Santa Fe Photographic Workshops. My summer in New Mexico with you changed my life. Thank you to my Santa Fe sisters: Taylor Auriel, Lisa Cates, McKenzie Leek, Julia C. Martin, Christi Wiltenburg, and Leah Woodruff. Also to Amanda Fine, Chantel Harvey, Gwendolyn Mercer, Jordan Cole, and Jud Davis. You provided a space of healing for me in front of the camera, what an incredible gift. Thank you to everyone at B&H Foto and Electronics, Bozeman Camera & Repair Inc, The Camera Shop of Santa Fe, Canon, Carters Camera Cottage, The Curated Fridge, Diversified Lab, Filter Photo Festival, F-Stop Magazine, Glazer's Camera, Holga, I Love Texas Photo, Instagram, Kodak, Lightbox

Photographic Gallery, Medium Photo Festival, Nikon, NJC Printing, Photo-eye, Precision Camera and Video, Schiller's Camera Company, and Southeastern Camera.

Our National Parks,

My heartfelt gratitude goes out to the National Park Service. Having the opportunity to see each grand landscape across the country was freeing and absolutely crucial to my healing. To each staff member, seasonal employee, volunteer, concessionaire, and vendor that assisted my travels, your smiles had the ability to turn my day around. Fellow hikers and friends I met along the trails, your companionship and bright energy kept me going.

Special mention to everyone at Big Bend National Park in Texas. Having visited at three pivotal times during my adventure, I "found my park" in every sense. My journey of writing these thoughts on paper began there on the birthday trip described in the chapter, "I Hear You".

Thank you Yellowstone Forever and Bob and Connie Landis for offering the Landis Artist-In-Residence program at Yellowstone National Park in Montana and Wyoming. My first official artist residency in the world's first National Park, it felt so right. My journey to completing these pages was made possible during my time of rest and rejuvenation there. It couldn't have been a more perfect opportunity and end to the adventure.

I now live my life as an advocate and promoter of our national parks. Everyone, get an annual pass if you're able and find a way to get involved. There is magnificent beauty in our own backyard! Find out more at www.nps.gov.

Music & Podcasts

99% Invisible, Absolutely Nothing Going On, The After Life, America's National Parks Podcast, This American Life, Apple Music, Audible, Austin City Limits, Bethel Church Sermon of the Week, Tara Brach, Create If Writing, The Current Minneapolis, Dear Sugars, DJ Cassandra, Happy Healthy Caregiver, Hidden Brain, Insights at the Edge, Journey To Manifesting with Sarah Prout, KDHX St. Louis, KEXP Seattle, Love Letter, Magic Lessons with Elizabeth Gilbert, Spotify, Strategic Hype, Super Soul, SXSW, The Totems, Unlocking Us with Brené Brown, Wortkunst Predigt, and Zen Studies Podcast

Spiritual Guides
Auric Visions, Austin Shambhala Center, Bible Study Fellowship, #Bible Verse of the Day, Blue Turtle Intuitive Counseling, Calm, Conscious Coaching by Julie, Cosmic Connections, DailyOM, Downtown Cornerstone Church, Gateway Church Austin, Grounded Mind with David Gandelman, Hillsong Sweden, Insight Timer, Jolie Dawn, Lee Harris Energy, My Grit, Grace + Gratitude, Mystic Valley, Nature's Treasures, Olive Tree Bible App, Priestess Paradigm, Providence Presbyterian Church, Qoya, It's Raining Zen, Singing Bird Coaching, Trece Spalten: Intuition & Healing, Wisdom Botanicals, and World Tapping Circle

Travel Services
Alaska Airlines, Amazon Kindle, American Airlines, AutoZone, CarMax, Chevrolet, Corky's Auto Supply, Delta Air Lines, Esurance, Eurail, Facebook, Firestone, Greyhound, Good Carma Auto, Google Maps, Husky Travel Centers, Jersey State Bank, Love's Travel Stops, McDonalds WiFi, O'Reilly Auto Parts, Pilot Flying J, Progressive, SkyView Lite, Southwest Airlines, Starbucks WiFi, Telle Tire & Auto, Terlingua Auto, Tires Plus, Toyota, TravelCenters of America, Trucker Path, U.S. Department of Transportation, and Yellowstone Dino Lube & Repair

Wellness
Al-Anon, Barnes-Jewish Hospital, Care and Counseling, The Caregiving Effect LLC, Divine Wellness Community, Games for Humanity, GriefShare, Healing Arts Center, Mercy Heartprints, MyFirstCancer.com, National Caregiving Conference, Planned Parenthood, Share Pregnancy and Infant Loss Support, Sherer Chiropractic Center, Siddha Labs, Siteman Cancer Center, Soma Vida, Sounds True, Wellness with Ashaleah, Women Making Waves, Your Life, Styled, and YMCA

Yoga
Back Trap Yoga, A Balanced Life with FitNikki, Black Lagoon: Art + Yoga, Black Swan Yoga, Blue Sky Yoga St. Louis, Dark Yoga Austin, Mangala Yoga, Mindful Movements, Pints and Poses Yoga, Practice Yoga Austin, River Bend Yoga, Roots To Wings Yoga and Healing, Santa Fe THRIVE, Shine Yoga, Studio Gaia, Wanderlust, Yoga Buzz, Yoga For All By Samantha, Yoga With Jamie, and Yokibics

Transformational Books

Thank you to the writers of the following titles for the opportunity to learn from your beautiful words and for giving me the inspiration to tell my own story. I highly recommend each one.

1. *The Alchemist* by Paulo Coelho
2. *Ansel Adams: Our National Parks* by William A. Turnage and Andrea G. Stillman
3. *The Art of Happiness: A Handbook for Living* by Dalai Lama
4. *The Artist's Way: A Spiritual Path to Higher Creativity* by Julia Cameron
5. *Big Magic: Creative Living Beyond Fear* by Elizabeth Gilbert
6. *Broken Open: How Difficult Times Can Help Us Grow* by Elizabeth Lesser
7. *Canyon Solitude: A Woman's Solo River Journey Through the Grand Canyon* by Patricia C. McCairen
8. *Codependent No More: How to Stop Controlling Others and Start Caring for Yourself* by Melody Beattie
9. *Desert Solitaire: A Season in the Wilderness* by Edward Abbey
10. *Don't Sweat the Small Stuff… and It's All Small Stuff: Simple Ways to Keep the Little Things from Taking Over Your Life* by Richard Carlson
11. *Emotional Agility: Get Unstuck, Embrace Change, and Thrive in Work and Life* by Susan David
12. *Finding Meaning: The Sixth Stage of Grief* by David Kessler
13. *The Four Agreements: A Practical Guide To Personal Freedom (A Toltec Wisdom Book)* by Don Miguel Ruiz
14. *The Gifts of Imperfection: Let Go of Who You Think You're Supposed to Be and Embrace Who You Are* by Brené Brown
15. *A Grief Observed* by C.S. Lewis
16. *Grief Unseen: Healing Pregnancy Loss through the Arts* by Laura Seftel
17. *Hold Still: A Memoir With Photographs* by Sally Mann
18. *It's Easier Than You Think: The Buddhist Way to Happiness* by Sylvia Boorstein
19. *Letter to My Daughter* by Maya Angelou

20. *The Life-Changing Magic of Tidying Up: The Japanese Art of Decluttering and Organizing* by Marie Kondo
21. *Love Warrior: A Memoir* by Glennon Doyle
22. *Moonlight Gratitude: 365 Nighttime Meditations For Deep, Tranquil Sleep All Year Long* by Emily Silva
23. *My Dakota* by Rebecca Norris Webb
24. *The Path To Love: Spiritual Strategies for Healing* by Deepak Chopra
25. *The Power of Now: A Guide to Spiritual Enlightenment* by Eckhart Tolle
26. *Rand McNally Road Atlas* by Rand McNally
27. *Tao Te Ching* by Laozi and Stephen Mitchell
28. *A Thousand-Mile Walk to the Gulf* by John Muir
29. *The Universe Has Your Back: Transform Fear to Faith* by Gabrielle Bernstein
30. *Upstream: Selected Essays* by Mary Oliver
31. *The Way of the Traveler: Making Every Trip a Journey of Self-Discovery* by Joseph Dispenza
32. *When Breath Becomes Air* by Paul Kalanithi
33. *When Things Fall Apart: Heart Advice for Difficult Times* by Pema Chödrön
34. *Wherever You Go, There You Are: Mindfulness Meditation in Everyday Life* by Jon Kabat-Zinn
35. *Wild: From Lost to Found on the Pacific Crest Trail* by Cheryl Strayed
36. *The Year of Magical Thinking* by Joan Didion
37. *Your Brightest Life Journal: A Creative Guide to Becoming Your Best Self* by Caroline Kelso Zook

Rachel and Maude in Badlands National Park, South Dakota

about the author

Rachel Helden is an artist from St. Louis, Missouri. *Free Way: An Adventure Through Loss* is a labor of love project that took about five years to live and write. After undergoing some fresh losses, her grandfather, a few dear friends, and two painful miscarriages, she pursued the self-publishing of these pages. (Thank you Grandpa Ray, Dave, Patti, Harmony, and Roland for the inspiration.) Perhaps her story can offer some relief, to give its readers an outlet to see the world and remember that they are not alone in grief.

Rachel studied Photography at School of Visual Arts in New York (MFA) and Ringling College of Art and Design in Florida (BFA). Her work experiences include Santa Fe Photographic Workshops, St. Louis Cardinals, and she was a Landis Artist-in-Residence at Yellowstone National Park with Yellowstone Forever.

Connect with Rachel on Instagram @_photonomad_ and find out more about her work on her website at www.RachelHelden.com.

plates